A POACHER'S TALE

Alf Curtis was born of a line of poachers into a poaching family, and learned the poacher's skills almost as soon as he could walk. His early schooling was a disaster, and he ended up in the dreaded Truant School, an experience which left permanent scars; but in the end he learned to read and write before he left school at fourteen. Although he worked at a variety of jobs, he could never keep away from the countryside and from rabbiting, birdcatching or poaching for long. His memoirs cover every kind of exploit, from ratting to the early days of greyhound racing, and range over the many different skills he acquired in the course of a restless life on the edge of London and Essex, from the countryman's familiarity with nets and snares to toymaking and watch-mending. When the book first appeared a reviewer called it 'almost a standard text on the art of poaching . . . *A Poacher's Tale* is not a book for the chicken-hearted: it has its roots in an unchained, full-blooded world of the past.' But it is more than that: like the other great poaching autobiography, *I Walked by Night*, it is the self-portrait of a remarkable character.

A POACHER'S TALE

Told by A. T. Curtis
Related by Fred. J. Speakman

THE BOYDELL PRESS

© Fred. J. Speakman and Alfred Curtis 1960
First published by G. Bell & Sons Ltd 1960
First published in COUNTRY LIBRARY 1983
by The Boydell Press
an imprint of Boydell & Brewer Ltd
PO Box 9, Woodbridge, Suffolk, IP12 3DF

Reprinted 1986

ISBN 0 85115 211 2

Printed in Great Britain by
St Edmundsbury Press Ltd, Bury St Edmunds, Suffolk

IN MEMORY OF MY MOTHER, WHOSE WISH IT WAS THAT
HER SON SHOULD WRITE THE STORY OF HIS LIFE

A. T. C.

Contents

		PAGE
	Introduction	ix
CHAPTER		
1.	I am Born to a Poaching Family	1
2.	I Go to School	12
3.	Freedom Again	28
4.	I Take Work	50
5.	The Poaching Life	70
6.	Of Rats and Ratting	85
7.	Of Fish and Fishing	102
8.	Of Divers Things Done	119
9.	The Bird-catcher	136
10.	I Meet with the Law	146
11.	I am Caught Again	152
12.	Of Greyhounds and Toys	159
13.	A Poacher Dreams	174
14.	Odd Thoughts and Explanations	179
	Appendix	189

Frontispiece A. T. Curtis *From a drawing by John Avis*

Introduction

HOW does one get to know a poacher and his story?
I went into a shop to buy gentles.
'Fishing?'
'No, I want them for a bat, a tame one.' I fetched Noccy from under my coat where he had made the journey.
'Don't you let that thing get near me!' I had no choice, Noccy flew straight on to Mrs. Curtis. And so I came to know Sally and Alf.

I went into the shop again and again. I listened to Alf discoursing with knowledge and authority on fishing topics. I heard tales of his past, and came to guess something of the richness of the life he had lived. One day he ended, 'I wish somebody would put it in a book for me before it's too late.'

'I will!' I said, and there and then we agreed to do it.

I have learnt a lot of 'the other side' of natural history since then, and am glad to have had the chance.

Whatever is spoken of as being a part of Alf's life, I believe. What he says he can do, he can. He will twist a piece of copper wire and a spring into a bird trap as he talks to you over the counter. He will sit at a sewing machine and hold his own be it at sewing or repairing. He will make a fishing rod while you stand and watch, and fit it with every gadget you can wish, and every one made with his own hands.

Whatever is told in this book is told in the belief that it is true. Where unpleasant things are said of others they are related without ill-will. They are included because they are an integral part of the man's life, of the boyhood that helped to mould him, of the fortunes and the misfortunes that befell him later. What is related here is a richness of life few men can equal. Telling it has been a long task and an arduous one; but a satisfying one.

FRED. J. SPEAKMAN

30th November, 1959

I am Born to a Poaching Family

1893 saw me born in the Rumbling Place, the Cattle Market of WalTham Abbey in Essex. (Yes, you pronounce the T.) The Place was little altered when last I saw it. The rails of the cattle pens are still there, and the drinking trough for the animals at the far end put up by the Lord of the Manor, and the little houses with their straight fronts, that stand almost on the pens, and look upon the Market. In one of these small houses I was born; and when Mother opened the door on a Tuesday, which was market day, there looking in would be the two big eyes of a cow, or the almond eyes of sheep, a few yards from the door.

So I began with animals, as it were, and all my life I've been with them.

Father was a gamekeeper, and when he lost that job – for poaching? it might have been, in fact, as like as not, he turned poacher in earnest. He had to, with eleven of us to feed. I began to learn from him early, as soon in fact as I could manage to walk far enough to go with him. When I was big enough to carry them, I had to take the tools of his trade, his decoy birds, his nets and his cartridges. Like all good keepers and poachers Father made his own cartridges, buying nothing but the cases, and those he used three or four times over, till they became useless.

Evening was the time for the making up of the cartridges, and I used to sit and watch him. When they were finished he would put them in the oven to dry. Mother always found an excuse to be out that night. Later on I came to making my own, filling them with whatever shot I wanted for the purpose in hand.

Father, as I have said, was a poacher, but he was a sportsman too. Every bird or creature that we shot had to be stalked – no sitting targets for us, and we had to kill outright. Stalk, shoot, and kill. It was our wits and skill against the wild.

The hardest birds to shoot, Father always said, were a snipe zigzagging off the mud, and a lark going up zigzag from the green of a field of clover. He should know, for he was a fine shot, was Father.

I remember once, my Uncle Archer was too ill to take his place in a shooting match. Father hadn't entered, he hadn't the money for the entry fee. So Uncle asked him to stand in for him, and Father accepted. Twenty pounds and a silver tea service he got out of that, about the last match I think he ever went to. Except one. For afterwards Father said he would challenge anyone from eighty miles around to a shooting match. When the day came he out-shot all comers, even though he was using two-and-a-half-inch cartridges, while the runner-up had three-inch, which carried a longer way.

I was only a boy, but I was in some of those old shooting matches, though not with a gun. I used to catch sparrows and starlings with a copper-wire trap. They were the targets, live ones. I'd catch thirty or forty sparrows and starlings in a week. Then on the day I'd go to the shooting field and lay out flower pots, with a string attached to each, and a bird under each pot. When the men came up for practice, they'd say, 'All right, son,' and I'd pull a string and release a bird. They had to shoot it in the air, to fall within a circle on the ground. A halfpenny each they would give me for the birds, and an extra sixpence for a treat. I took the money home, for there was never too much coming in. Not that money really bothered us; it came, and it went; where the next might come from we never knew. The two things that did matter, were food and clothes, and food came first. With Father the shot he was, we were seldom poor at mealtimes. He would bring home rabbits and hares, and birds of varied kind, pheasants and duck,

I AM BORN TO A POACHING FAMILY

partridge and plover and snipe, anything edible. Mother roasted them at once, no leaving them to get half-rotten first; besides, we were too hungry to wait.

When I was not in the fields or the woods with Father, I was doing something on my own. Boys of my day had to make their own amusements, and find their own interests. As like as not, I'd be fishing.

We had moved to Baker's Entry by then, a narrow cul-de-sac off Paradise Row, where the cottages stand but a few yards back from the water. I fell in so often – it wasn't very deep – that in the end they tied me to a post. The post was still there till a year or so ago. Now it's gone, and railings have been put up before the cottages. From the post I used to fish. When I caught one I yelled, and Mother came and took it off the hook for me. If it was big enough to fry, four to six inches, she dropped it into a pan of salt water, killing and salting it at the same time. She fried her fish in duck fat; she had a bladder of it always hanging ready. And as I fished, from overhead would come the sound of the bells of Waltham Abbey, to me the most peaceful sound in all the world, and full, like life, of hidden mysteries.

Evening brought fishing too, of a special kind.

A tunnel with a grating at the entrance ran under the road, leading to the Abbey. There was little water in the tunnel till near dusk, when the sluices were opened up-river and the water came down. With the water came the fish – perch and chub, great big fellows among them, and the fishermen used to line up early, ready for them. I'd take off my shoes, roll up my trousers, and drop the four or five feet down from the bridge into the water on the tunnel side of the railings. Then they'd pass their lines down to me, with a big lob worm on each hook, and I'd lay them out in the shallow water under the road, all trim and neat, ready for the big fish to come down. An hour, maybe two hours, the men waited on top, holding the ends of their lines. One bite was all they could get: I got a penny a line.

Sometimes I went evening fishing with Father, for perch. At least, we made ready for catching them. For when Father knew he was going for perch, big ones, in the deep water near the old Abbey Bridge, he would catch about two dozen minnows, and put them in a clean onion jar with a long string tied to it and holes punched in the lid.

Then, after dark, we'd go out and lower the jar carefully into the river, and make the string fast where it would not be seen.

The next morning, at daybreak, we were there. Father had his old willow-stick (no rod for him) and there he fished with a minnow – outside the jar. All night the perch had been waiting round the jar for the chance of a minnow, now here was one, only it had Father's hook in it; and so we came home, with breakfast. That was in the old days, before any Town Hall stood in the road to watch our comings and our goings.

It wasn't fish alone we got out of the river. Sometimes there were floods, and then everything came down – beer bottles, crates, even a table and chairs. Father had a big hook on a long line, for throwing out. He didn't always catch what he wanted, of course, but in that way he got all the timber he needed, for Father could throw. Indeed, any outdoor sport came easily to him. Like the running.

One year there was a clock given by one of the pubs as a prize for an obstacle race. Moocher Walker said to Father – he was known to everyone as 'Moocher', being a thin disguise for poacher – well, Moocher said to Father, 'Doughy, we'll win that clock.' (Doughy, because he had done a bit of baking in his varied career.) 'But,' he went on, 'there's a crack runner from London coming down to take part in it, we'll have to think a bit.'

They laid their plans. Father, being the better runner, thin and tall, he was six feet two, was to run like a hare and be first under the tarpaulin, and first out.

He was. But Moocher so contrived it that he and the Londoner were under together. Then Moocher got up, and of course the tarpaulin drew so tight round the edges the Londoner could find no way out. Father won the race.

I suppose you'd call it dishonest, yet it wasn't simply that we wanted the clock; there was a spirit in those days in a place like Waltham, you just didn't let outsiders walk away with what was yours. There was a real feeling of community:

I AM BORN TO A POACHING FAMILY

everyone knew everybody, we put up with the bad, we enjoyed the good. Uncle Lonzo was an example. He had a temper, a bad one, and yet he was a good man.

He came in one day, after three or four drinks too many – that was his failing – and fell into the armchair.

'Where's my dinner?' he yelled at Grandmother.

'I'm getting it, you'll have to wait.'

During the waiting he fell fast asleep. Grandma hadn't had her dinner either, so she set to and ate his. But when it came to the eggs, she softly smeared some round his whiskers, and over his waistcoat.

Uncle Lonzo stirred at last. 'Where's my dinner?' he shouted.

'Why, you've eaten it!' replied Grandma.

'Eaten it! I'VE EATEN IT!'

'Well, if you don't believe me, look at yourself in the glass.'

'And I don't remember a d——d thing about it,' muttered Uncle to the glass.

Yet, as I've said, he was a good man out of his cups. Every year, when Fair Day came round, and the roundabouts and the swings were put up in the Square, he would walk in.

'Nance,' he would call to my mother, 'fetch the children.' Off we would go to the Fair, with the pubs handy all around, and Lonzo keeping away from them all. First, it was the roundabouts, a penny a ride. Then straight across from the Fair, Uncle Lonzo took us, to the shoe shop, where he bought us each a pair of hobnailed boots, one and eleven to two and eleven a pair. There were eleven of us, remember. He'd stay with Mother a day or two perhaps, or he might go straight off and we wouldn't see him again for a whole twelve-month.

Drink was his trouble, to the end.

One day Father was crossing the Market Place on his way back from a walk with his gun. There in the middle of the Place was Uncle Lonzo, disgracing the family: drunk, holding up half a crown in his hand and bawling, 'These don't grow on trees! These don't grow on trees!'

Father ran to the nearest pub, The Green Dragon, and stood his gun in a corner. Then coming up behind Lonzo he threw him over his shoulder and, not wanting a crowd, carried him down Quaker's Lane, where we lived at the time. He stood him down beside the door, mighty out of breath. 'Coo,' says Lonzo, 'is that you, Doughy? I did enjoy that ride!' Father hadn't, nor had he enjoyed seeing him in the Market, and he set to and tried to knock some sense into him. They both lost their tempers then, and there was a terrible row, and Uncle Lonzo swore he would shoot Father. He came indoors, loaded a muzzle-loader and stood it in the corner. This time he stayed with us for two months. He never used the gun on Father, of course, but he had begun to go wrong in the head. Twice he shot his own shadow coming down the stairs, thinking it was a burglar. In the end they took him away to the asylum.

Some strange things happened with guns in our family. When Grandfather was eighty-nine, he was unloading a muzzle-loader, pulling out the charge with the worm on the end of the ramrod. The gun went off. It blew a piece of his forehead away and he lived for eight days, as Grandmother always told, with his brain showing. The blast took a piece from his eyebrow ridge, and as Grandmother was bending over cooking, the piece of bone fell down her bosom.

I have told you that Father made his own cartridges. He made a special one for the deer. Over the years our family had sampled red deer, roe, and fallow, all from Epping Forest. Later the roe died out, and the red were taken away because of the havoc they committed, but not before our family had had its share. To make a deer cartridge Father would melt lead into one of Mother's steel thimbles. When he turned it out, he had a casting shaped something like a little flower-pot. He fitted it into the top of a twelve-bore cartridge, packed it round with paper, put a wad on top and turned over the rim of the cartridge, and it was ready for a smooth-bore barrel. These things came easy to Father, and he had the tools for the job. One bullet killed a deer outright. It made a small hole where it went in, but a gaping one where it came out. That meat Father sold up in Town, never locally. 'Black mutton' it was known as by all in the game. Young as I was, I had a hand in that too. Whenever there was any black mutton to be disposed of, I was told to fetch the cart from the back of a little pub. No, I'm not telling its name, but it was Waltham way, be sure.

One evening there came word that Father had got a deer down in the woods. I started off to run for the cart. Tearing round a haystack in the dark, I fell over a sleeping donkey. I didn't know it was a donkey, all I felt was fur, and that was enough. I bolted, and the hobnails of my boots must have been red-hot with the speed I made. I never did reach the pub. In the early hours of next morning I was found miles away, wandering about with no idea where I'd got to.

There were times when Father was not able to use his gun. A lot of business went on in pawnbrokers' shops in those days, and Father made many a visit.

One time when he was out of work, he pawned his gun. Then somebody gave him an old muzzle-loader that had lost its hammer. Father didn't bother to get one, he simply loaded up, and took with him a crony with hand well bandaged in a piece of rag, and holding a lump of iron. Father would come into the field where the rabbits were, stalk them, put a cap on the gun, and take aim. While the gun was at his shoulder, his pal would lean over. 'Hit it!' Father would hiss, and George would smack down on the cap: and many a rabbit they brought home shot in that way, without a hammer on the gun.

Before Father got his gun back, the pawnbroker's son was asked to shoot a mad bull. Father saw him going. 'What, shooting?' he asked, quizzing down at the gun.

'Yes, a mad bull.'

'I'll come with you,' said Father. They went together, and the bull was shot.

Coming home, Father said, 'That's a nice gun you've got. Mind if I have a look at it?'

'Certainly.'

'Ah,' says Father, 'a very nice gun indeed. And now you can go home and tell Father that Mr. Curtis has got his own gun back!'

And he had too, for the ticket had not run out. When the pawnbroker came round for the gun, Father simply said, 'I left this gun in your charge for safe keeping, and you know, and I know, that you had no right whatever to let anyone shoot with it.' And he kept the gun.

Father didn't always have to use a gun to get meat. Going through the woods one day, that is, through Epping Forest, he came upon a deer with a fawn just dropped, a fallow deer new-born.

Quick as thought, Father whipped out his knife and slit the fawn's left hind foot down to the quick – crippled it so that it could not escape. Three weeks he left it there, and then brought it home, and we ate it. Cruel? We did hard things; times were hard to us. It was no worse than goes on every day in the slaughter-house where your meat is prepared. If Father were hard-pushed for a piece of 'black mutton', then he could always obtain it. A certain Keeper kept him supplied with Forest deer, for even a Keeper might have his price – and that black mutton, shot at one in the afternoon, would be hanging in a London market by six the next morning.

We worked often in the bitter nights, with mustard and wool inside our boots to keep our feet from freezing, and a sheet of brown paper with a hole in it for the head to go through, worn as a vest to keep the wind out – but this Keeper had his game all ready on his doorstep as it were, under his own protection. He would watch out where the deer were coming to feed, and there lay out provender for them. Then, coming secretly, he would drive them in a panic of fear straight for the wires or scaffold lines he had strung among the trees. Many a carcase of black mutton went to London Market of his doing, and many a full meal he enjoyed himself, of venison from deer whose legs he had snapped. He was never caught, for once the lines were hidden away, there remained nothing to tell the tale.

Then Father found a helper who could kill a deer as well as any man, and say never a word about it. He bought a dog, a young greyhound, and he soon began to find out things about it.

In Waltham, by the Market, there lived a cat, a large lop-eared cat that was afraid of no dog. One day when Father was going through, it leaped out on to the back of Father's dog, scared it with the suddenness of the attack and was away before the dog could retaliate.

Father got the dog under control, then turned to the woman who owned the cat: 'If ever,' he warned, 'my dog comes this way again, you be careful of your cat!'

Not many months after, Father was passing again through Quaker Lane where the cat lived, with the dog off the lead. The cat sat on a doorstep, unmoving.

In one bound the dog left Father's heels. The cat fled in terror, through the open door into the kitchen, the dog after it; and there he killed it, under the kitchen table. It caused a terrible row in Waltham, for everyone knew the cat and admired it. But Father held his talk: he had seen the possibilities of the dog.

He'd heard of a hare on Matt Bott's farm, a hare no dog could catch, though many had tried. One Sunday morning Father took a stroll that way, with his dog. 'What are you up to, Doughy?' asked the farmer.

'I've come to try the dog at the old hare I hear so much about,' says Father. Matt laughs.

'He'll never catch him, too many have tried and failed. But you have a go.'

So Father strolled through the fields, and after about a quarter of an hour he put the hare up. The dog went away, and coursed it. He came back with the tail of the hare in his mouth, all he could get; and Father and Matt stood and laughed over it. But through all his laughter Father was thinking how near the dog had got. He was back the following Sunday, and put up the hare again, and again the dog coursed it. This time he came back with the body of the hare.

That dog, had he been alive today, would have been a champion. I know, I've trained many a racing greyhound since those days. It was a joy to see him go. When he leaped a stile or a gate, there were his four feet together on the top of the post, and he was gone, like the wind itself.

Then Father found out something more about Scandalous Jack, as he'd named the dog. Father, Moocher and Jack were going through Epping Forest after a rabbit or two, when suddenly the dog pricked up his ears. The men could see nothing.

'Go to it, boy!' whispered Father, and the dog was gone.

Father waited and whistled for his return. Not for some time did Jack turn up, and when he did there was blood all over his chops. He led the men back a good mile through the woods and there, stretched on the ground, lay a deer, dead.

Now he knew what Jack was capable of, Father kept him and trained him for deer-killing and nothing else. In the two years before he parted with him to an uncle, many and many a deer was killed for the London markets.

I heard of all these doings, even when I had no part in them. It was a good introduction to the poaching life.

There were other things we killed beside the deer.

Father used to take me with him on the 'Mash', Waltham Mash – yes, I suppose it's 'marsh' really: a wonderful place for a boy, a green and level stretch where the larks hung overhead in the summer to sing, and in winter the snipe went up from the river-side.

One day Father winged a goose, and brought it down. He tied it down to look as if it was feeding, and he shot the other three as they came in one after the other to investigate. They were the only geese I ever remember to be shot on the Mash.

Even for birds we did not always need a gun. Father had a net on two long poles, a back-net for catching sparrows in the ivy of houses. It was poaching, of course, for we asked no permission, but just went after dusk when the birds were in for the night.

Then we had a scare. One night we'd laid the net against the ivy, folded it together, and taken out the birds. We went softly round the corner and began again. Just as we closed the net, an old woman poked her head out of the window, wondering what on earth she could hear. She didn't have a chance to find out, and we didn't stay to tell her. She was in the net. We had to lay off bird-netting for some time after that, for the police were on the look-out.

And so the years of my boyhood came and went, with more adventures than fall to most boys, and all the time I was learning; learning that if times grew hard, I could live off the country. There was much country around Waltham then, more than you will find today, with so much of it built upon.

But all things must end.

I AM BORN TO A POACHING FAMILY

There came a time when Father went out to try some new powder – green powder it was, supposed to have come all the way from India. Father didn't really know how to use it, but he was game to find out. So he loaded up a cartridge in the usual way, as for black powder, and he fired it on the Mead in Waltham, on a Sunday morning. He blew the gun into five bits, and the rib, the strip that runs between the two barrels, curled up like a clock spring. Father spun round like a spinning top with the repercussion, before he fell.

He went to hospital, and down came the experts, to try to find out what powder had been through the gun. They never found out, or if they did, kept their counsel; and just as well. Green powder it was, all the way from India, but by way of the Powder Mills, where Father was working at the time.

Yet I remember him as a good man, and a sportsman. All he did, his poaching of all kinds, he did for the sake of his family.

Now he was laid up for eight weeks, and all the time we were getting poorer, for there was no relief of any kind for us. Because of that shooting, Mother had to sell her home, for practically nothing, to a dealer. Houses in those days were cheap.

I was sent to my aunt in Tottenham. There I came to the age of eleven and was sent to school for the first time. But I could not stay at school, because of the wild life that was in me, the fishing, and the poaching, and the green places.

I Go to School

MY aunt sent me to Coleraine Park School, and so at the age of eleven I began my book-learning, and found it so novel that I settled down well.

However, it wasn't very many weeks before Mother had got a new home together. It may seem incredible in these times, when hundreds of thousands of new houses have been built and yet there is shortage everywhere, that Mother experienced no difficulty at all in finding a house to live in. So long as the rent could be found, a house was always waiting. And Father had found a new job, as a scaffolder. Before long I was home again.

Every morning Father would be off, wearing clothes that were the hall-mark of his trade: flap-corduroy trousers (bought from the local pawn-shop, the only place in Waltham where he could buy them), a scaffolding belt, and hobnailed boots.

Father was very particular about those boots. He declared you could tell the status of a scaffolder by the shine on his boots. So it was my job every night before I went to bed, to clean Father's. There was no such thing in our house as boot polish. We used blacking, Day and Martin's, at a farthing a cake. It was moistened with a little vinegar or water, and rubbed on. Then came the polishing – and only elbow grease would make a shine. There was some polishing to do, for Father had to see his face in the boots before he was satisfied. I got my wages for it, of course: a penny a week; and I earned that penny.

I GO TO SCHOOL

Hearing I'd been to a school, Father sent me to another, but the novelty had worn off, and I could not settle down again. I began to play truant, to stay away from school without permission, a very common thing in those early days, and one that always brought punishment, if found out.

I was found out, and the biggest hiding I ever had for truanting, my Father gave me. He came to the school, and was told of all my absences; and there and then he took off his belt, his scaffolder's belt, and laid about me, nor did he rest till we reached home.

There I collapsed, and was carried up to bed and undressed. Mother called for Father to come up. 'You see what you've done to him?' she said in a low voice. Father looked. I was turning blue and green and yellow all over my back. Father was deeply upset, for he loved us all. 'I'll never hit him again,' he vowed, and he kept his word. On occasion, when he had cause, and that was all too often, I've seen his hand raised in sudden anger, and then his face change, and the hand drop.

Instead, he'd send me to bed without a meal; but I knew, and he must have known, that Mother would never let us go hungry, that before long she would steal up with a tray of good food.

Sometimes, as a treat, Father would take me with him to work on a Saturday morning. We'd go together up to St. Thomas's Hospital, where Father had his job as scaffolder. Once there, he would say, 'Now you go and have a look at London – see a few of the shops, and be back here at twelve o'clock.'

I was always back on time, waiting for him to come from work.

'Come on, boy,' he'd say as he caught sight of me, 'let's go to the Market.' He meant Smithfield Market.

There he would buy meat for the family; half a dozen rabbits, perhaps, at sixpence each. The very best, they had to be, for Father who had shot and snared so many knew a good rabbit when he saw one. But often enough, he would walk around, looking at the meat, and then go up to the butcher he'd decided on, and buy a whole pluck – the inside of an animal, liver, lights and heart – for ninepence the lot.

Then we'd come home, and Father would go out to hang his purchase in the coolest place we had – in the wash-house.

Next morning, being Sunday, and a free day, Father was up first and went out quietly to the wash-house, and there cut off what he wanted to cook for breakfast.

With a good settled home again, I suppose I should have been happy at school, learning all I could, but I remembered all the wild days we had known together as boys, and the days, and the nights, out with Father and his friends. Despite all the warnings I'd been given, I started to play truant in earnest. I stayed away from school, and kept away from home as much as I could. I fell in with some boys from Waltham Abbey, boys well up in the art of looking after themselves. They showed me a way to keep myself for days, or even weeks.

'All you need,' they said, 'is a couple of shillings to start you off. Then we'll go down to Clarke, Nichols & Coombe and lay in a stock of Rowland's cough sweets.'

I borrowed the money from home, and off I went. Thirty-six packets of Rowland's Cough Tablets we bought for our two shillings.

I was up before daybreak, and making my way to Finsbury Park Tube Station. It was the season of coughs and colds. I took up my stand outside the station. If I heard anyone give so much as a cough, I was after him like a shot. 'Rowland's Cough Tablets, Penny a Packet!' I'd shout. And two out of three bought a packet.

On every thirty-six packets I made a shilling. So long as the bad weather lasted, I was assured of a good sale. The first two shillings I made went home to repay the debt. After all, a shilling then was a lot of money. You could buy a ha'porth of tea, a ha'porth of sugar, a ha'porth of marg, a ha'porth of anything. In those days, when a halfpenny was a useful coin of the realm, a shilling would keep our family in good food for a whole day.

But now that I knew I could earn a shilling in a morning or at most two mornings, I began to have other ideas, for always I wanted the freedom of the fields.

Some boys told me that at The Tuns public house there was a big owl kept in a cage on the counter, and they were wanting

I GO TO SCHOOL

sparrows for the owl, a penny for a live bird, a halfpenny dead. I knew how to catch sparrows, I'd caught dozens of them for the target shooting, in brick traps, and copper-wire traps specially made.

I knew where I could buy them too; in The Boundary, that runs between Edmonton and Tottenham. They hung in bundles outside an ironmonger's, with many another trap. I bought two, at a penny each.

At last I could move away from the places where everyone could see me, and where at any moment I might be caught for truanting. I could go back to the open lands where I belonged.

The open land, then, was Ploughman's Brick Field: a place full of adventure and romance and interest for a boy. There I baited my traps with a piece of bread, and set them in the grasses. Today people throw bread all over the place in waste, but a piece of bread then was a treat for a sparrow. I didn't have long to wait. A sparrow would come, hover a second, and drop down to take a peck. I'd catch seven or eight in a morning, some alive, some dead where the wire had struck them a blow on the head.

Other boys soon found what I was up to, of course, and they would come and crouch with me, hearing the wind whisper in the grasses, and the moving of a bird's wings as it came.

When we'd caught enough, we put them into a little cloth bag, and off we went to The Tuns, to draw the blood-money. This was easy living, I thought. As long as the owl on the counter lived I need never starve, nor need I appear too near school.

I even had money to spare for evenings. I'd go down to The Gaff, the tuppenny hop, as we knew it, a little theatre where snug in the warmth of the gallery I could see a whole play through for twopence.

And coming out after, with my head full of dreams, I would feel the night air strike chill, and hear the wind blowing far off, and a bird in the sky perhaps; and I'd sleep out, under the open sky, so long as the wind was held from me.

This was all right when the weather was fine, but that wasn't always. So I picked out two of the boys I knew, and told them what I planned. We would gather bricks from about the field and make a little house where we could sleep at night, and where we could keep our things during the day, and do our cooking. They agreed and we set to.

We chose a waste piece of ground, where nobody else ever came, and where the hedges were close and a good screen, and yet we could see the open fields beyond. I had seen a picture of an Eskimo igloo and I would have liked to make one, but it wasn't easy in bricks. So we made it square, and we left out a brick or two for air.

Now there were three of us to keep, all truanting, and all young. We swore to keep together, and not to go back to school if we could help it. We pooled our ideas for making money. There was always the owl; there was the selling of cough sweets in the season; and to these we added the hawking of bootlaces, and the sale of roses for buttonholes, with any odd jobs that might come our way.

We'd buy our stock of laces in the day, twelve pairs a penny. Then in the evening we would make our round of the public houses.

We'd push open the door, and call, 'Mohair bootlaces, all strong and handy!' A penny for six, we sold them: we'd make between us as much as three shillings.

The rose selling was more ambitious. It meant that one of us must go up to Covent Garden, to buy the roses – a shilling's worth of broken heads, that is roses with broken stalks – some flower wire and some fern.

We had them finished by evening; wired, with a sprig of fern to back the bloom, and lovely they were. Everybody then wore a button-hole, and we had no difficulty in selling them at a penny each, with the shops and pubs open till eleven at night, and all the courting couples glad of the chance to buy.

Late at night we would stumble our way to the little house in the deserted corner of the brickfield; with the day and its adventures very real, and the night close and bright among the stars. Here, we felt, we could live for ever, secure and happy. Until one day we heard of something terrible that happened close by.

There were four little boys we knew by sight. They used to

I GO TO SCHOOL

cross the brickfield and go to the railway. There, in a large heap of shingly ballast, they had dug out a tunnel and were making a cave at the end of it.

One day when they were busy working in it, a passing train shivered the roof in and buried three of the boys alive; only one, who happened to be at the mouth of the tunnel, escaped.

All at once the brick house seemed less secure.

Supposing the same thing were to happen to us! We used to lie awake, frightening ourselves with talk about it, although we knew it to be impossible, and then lie awake again, hearing the strange haunting hoot of the owls, or the melancholy barking of a dog; and then the rumble of the train's oncoming. We thought of giving up our Eskimo home, but we could not.

At last, of course, our parents found where we were and what we were doing, and home we all went. What with Father's anger in his eyes, and Mother's tears, I know I promised to be a good boy, and go back to school and stay there. But when the morning shone white into my bedroom, and I smelled the breath of fields, and almost the scent of the river there, I couldn't, for all I'd meant what I'd said. I dressed quietly and slipped out, into the fresh world where only the sparrows were awake, and they sleepy along the gutters of houses.

But now somebody else was after me, the Attendance Officer, known to every boy as the School Board Man. Even the brickfield was no longer sanctuary, for he knew we had been there. So I found errands to run, and little jobs that would take me away from the field during the daylight hours. And since I knew they could catch me any time they wanted now, I used to sneak home whenever I thought Father was out, and see the family. Mother would give me food, some of whatever she had in the house, as if I had never been away at all. She would ask me where I had been the evening before, and how I had spent the night and what had happened to me since last I was home and what trouble was I in?

But the School Board Man didn't come, and in our feeling of safety, we all met again at the brick house in the field.

But time was catching up on us. All too soon we were to exchange the bright sunlight for grey slavery.

Before that happened, however, there occurred a little incident that was to colour the whole of my life.

There was a tea party being given at the Tabernacle in Langage Lane, Edmonton. We knew it well, for in the daytime helpers ran a soup kitchen there, and more than once we had gone along hopefully, and come away warm with soup. Afternoon saw us settled comfortably there, with bread and butter, cup of tea, and bun.

When it was all over, and cleared away, there was a call for somebody to go up and recite, and I volunteered. I always liked the sound of words, and I had a head for remembering them. So up I went on to the platform, and there I recited a poem my mother had taught me. 'Somebody's Mother'* it was called. I remember it to this day – and its lesson, 'Ever act kindly'.

I could tell they liked it, the way they all sat quiet. Then they burst out clapping. When it was all over, just as I was getting down from the platform, the Minister stopped me and asked for my name and address.

A fortnight later a book came to my home, a prize for my reciting.

I was not there. At last the School Board Man had really caught up. He had marched me off to the Police Station, where there was a warrant waiting, sending me away to a Truant School; a school of correction for truanters and other misfits. Now I was to give up the green grass and the golden sun, for dismal rooms set in a neighbourhood of mean streets, grey and unhappy as the life I was entered upon.

The kindly tolerance of home, the tears and the forgiveness, were exchanged for a life composed of blows and bitterness.

My arrival at the school set the tone for the rest of the stay. I was given a cup of cocoa and a piece of bread. When they were consumed, I was told to undress and make a bundle of my clothes. My last link with the outside world was gone. I was bathed in a great square bath, and given other clothes to wear; an old suit of brown corduroy, and old socks that had been darned till only a skeleton of original sock was left.

That was the only time I bathed there alone, and the only

* See Appendix

I GO TO SCHOOL

time I was not supervised. Normally we bathed in batches of twenty, with the Labour Master at the side looking on, wet towel in hand. As soon as he spotted any unwillingness to duck under, a shy new boy, or one who didn't like water, he would signal, and half a dozen boys, eager to hurt somebody weaker than themselves, would pounce and duck the unlucky boy: yes, and hold him under; till finally he was allowed to stand up and splutter and gasp for the breath that wouldn't come. As he stood up, the wet towel came across his bare back, 'Thwack!' and 'Thwack!' again; till the back was sore with blows. And so that boy learned that it was better in the long run to obey and duck under, rather than be ducked.

A hundred and twenty boys the school housed, at full strength. Six batches of twenty to be bathed. The Labour Master had his enjoyment, with the wet towel waiting, hovering around each.

I shall never forget nor forgive him, for all the unnecessary indignities and cruelties he inflicted upon us boys.

The longest day must come to an end, even in a Truant School. At bedtime we were marched off to the dormitories, beds in a line down each side of the room, like a hospital ward.

We were marched up in sections, in batches of eight. By the side of the bed we stood to attention, waiting to be told to undress.

Then, it was clothes off, fold, place at foot of bed, and wait for the order to get in. There weren't many dawdlers then, a minute saw us all settled.

Then came the next batch, till the dorm was full.

Lights out.

Silence.

Not a boy spoke. Not a word down the whole white length of the rows. Only later, under cover of the clothes, a boy might cry his heart out for home; while the lucky ones, not lately singled out for trouble, lay and dreamed awake of a different world where people lived and were happy. That time of bed was the only peace we knew in twenty-four hours.

At six, the new day began.

The doors were opened. 'All up! All up!' echoed down the room. Woe betide the boy who was a bit sluggish, he was marked down for punishment. The day's routine had begun.

First came bed inspection, as we stood to attention beside them. The slightest sign of wet on any bed and that boy must remain standing where he was.

For the rest, it was dress ready for washing. Downstairs we marched, still in eights, and out-doors to the wash-house to wash, with yellow soap and cold water, summer and winter.

Back again, still marching, but refreshed. We marched everywhere, even to the lavatories, eight boys to eight lavatories, all in the open and with half-doors.

We lined up in front of them. 'About turn!' 'In!' 'Out!'

Often there wasn't really time – but another eight were waiting – and pity the boy who had made the slightest error.

When washing was finished, off we went to the schoolroom, a place nearly as cold as the yard.

Now our day really began, of bullying and thrashing, of working and of learning.

There was, in every section of boys, a favourite, as always when punishments are hard. Now, while we waited, one or other of these boys would be called out, to tell tales of others, to get other boys a good hiding; though in all fairness let it be said that sometimes the sneak was punished himself.

While we waited, wondering whose turn it was today to be picked out, others, in worse plight, were waiting upstairs, standing to attention by their beds. Now their turn was coming. One of the favourites was called out and sent up to fetch the boys, and the beds.

When they came down, the bed, a palliasse, was strapped to its owner's back, and one by one the boys were marched out into the open. There, round the yard, with that heavy clumsiness fastened to his back, the boy must parade till his palliasse was dry.

Quite naturally it was most often the little boys who had to suffer, little mites scarcely able to stagger round with their beds. I was there myself a number of times, and saw. Even today, it makes my blood hot to think of the shame and the senseless brutality of it.

The bed-driers were not the only ones in the yard.

I GO TO SCHOOL

In the dormitories, four of them, stood twenty buckets, for the use of the boys in the night.

Every morning twenty boys were wanted for those twenty buckets. Any boy who had done the least thing wrong the previous day, such as smile across at his friend, or wink, or dare to move an inch when the class had been told to sit still, any boy who had unwittingly incurred the wrath of the Labour Master, was marked down for one of the buckets. The twenty were easy to find.

They stood there in the yard now, in a line: twenty boys each with a bucket at his feet; while the little boys stumbled round with their bedding.

Now each of the twenty was handed a long scrubbing brush.

And feet together, legs straight, they had to bend over and scrub that bucket. Scrub in half-hour shifts, half an hour for the near-side, then turn the bucket and scrub the other side for the next half-hour, or until seven o'clock.

Then, at last, we heard the order (Yes, I was on buckets, too), 'Fall in!' We stood up, or we tried to. 'Fall over!' would have been a better order. Our sense of balance was gone, we could only stumble about the place. It was two or three minutes before that bent back would straighten out. All the time the Labour Master stood laughing at our antics.

At last we were all in the schoolroom with the rest. There we sat, waiting while the duty boys laid breakfast in the dining hall.

Meals were as Spartan as the routine.

We marched in, and stood for Grace along the wooden tables, which were bare save for a piece of bread and a tin pannikin for each boy and large metal jugs of water. The tin had been scoured off the pannikins by much cleaning. If they were bright overnight they were often rusty by morning. Yet the half-dish of porridge they contained was like gold to our eyes. While we stood waiting, we were looking to see if a neighbour had a drop more porridge, or had been given a thicker slice of bread, for all the serving was performed by the unskilled hands of boys.

If we couldn't pick a place with a large helping, then we tried to get next to a new boy. We knew from long experience, that as soon as he tasted the porridge it would make him feel sick, and he would be unable to eat it. Then, if only the Labour Master wasn't looking, we'd help him by changing plates and get ourselves an extra breakfast.

But the Labour Master made a habit of looking into the tins of new boys; at the porridge, thin and watery or thick with lumps of uncooked oats the size of an egg.

The new boy would feel the Labour Master near. He would look up piteously. 'I, I can't eat it, sir!'

'Go out in front!' And out he would go before the whole school, any one of whom would gladly have eaten it, pannikin in one hand, spoon in the other.

'NOW,' said the Labour Master, 'eat it! EAT it!'

Look out if he didn't.

But eat it he usually did, with the porridge running out of the corner of his mouth. Not till the porridge was gone, could we drink our water – from the pannikins.

From breakfast we were taken out once more to the yard and paraded. There we were detailed for work. Eight for the kitchen, so many for the sewing room, so many more for cleaning and scrubbing and five for the darning room, where anything that could be called a garment was darned and darned again. Often the darning seemed a waste of time. One of my brothers – four of us went to the school altogether – made up his mind that some socks were beyond repair. He wasn't going to waste time on them, so he hid them up the chimney instead. Of course later on the socks were wanted and called for, and he was found out and got the hiding he had asked for.

There were other boys detailed for the boot-maker's shop. There they repaired boots for the boys, and for the staff. Only the best worker in the group would be entrusted with the repair of the staff boots – the Labour Master's and the Schoolmaster's. He used only the best material there was in the shop, and he had to take his time and make a good job of it. He knew what it meant if he didn't.

But any old piece of leather clumped on to a boot was good enough for the boys. And they didn't complain when the boots came back, if they did, for more than one boy was going

I GO TO SCHOOL

round with a ten on one foot and a nine on the other, and glad to do so and say nothing.

Those not detailed for this work went to lessons till dinner time.

Dinner was an improvement on breakfast – with an enamel plate in place of the pannikin. There were two potatoes, or three according to size, and always boiled in their skins, old or new. With them, and dwarfed by them, was our one small portion of meat.

There was cabbage, but only when those grown on the school ground were ready. And, of course, an abundance of water. But water alone is not a meal. The only time we could be sure of a full plate was when visitors came and stayed for dinner. They came all too seldom.

But in the summer, when the fruit was growing, there would be fallen apples from the orchard. We were allowed one each, picked from the wastepaper basket.

Sometimes, from somewhere, nuts appeared, and we were given them – as many as a boy could grasp in the finger-tips of one hand.

When the afternoon session began, the morning school boys changed places with the workers, and so the hours slipped round till it was time for tea.

Pannikins again, of cocoa, ship's cocoa, very strong, full of fat, and unsweetened. With it went a large slice of coarse brown bread, about an inch and a half thick. For butter, we dipped the bread into the cocoa.

Sometime in the evening came a half-hour for clothing complaints, a time when a boy might show a hole to see if it did indeed call for mending. If it did, there was a heap of old clothes that had been through the sewing room. Not that the boy was likely to find a fit; as with the boots, he took something near and wore it – in silence.

Once a week too, there was a laundry half-hour, for changing our clothes. The clean clothes were put in front of us, clean shirt and towel and vest, tied up with a striped handkerchief but with no mark to suggest ownership.

We changed there, and as we took off our old clothes they were inspected at once.

That was how they found out about the hiding I had been

given, when I had been punched in the back, and knocked, half senseless, against a form.

I held up my shirt. There, in the middle of the back, was a big clot of blood and pus.

'Turn round!' They wanted to see my back. I felt the fear creeping on them, and from them to me, for I knew it was bad, though I had said no word. They were frightened, and I knew it; for there, right on my spine, was a raw, ugly place. The scar is there to this day.

When next the doctor came on one of his regular visits, I was sent for, examined, and questioned. I told them I had knocked my back against a form. I wouldn't tell them the truth, so great was my fear of what would happen next, if I told. This punishment had been for nothing.

Yet some of the masters we had in school were kindly men. There was a music master. On three nights of every week we had singing, and part-singing at that. This music master was the kindest master we ever had. He couldn't understand us, and we, being so used to brutality, failed to understand him. We made his life one long torment, so that at the end of a month he left.

The Labour Master was a different breed. He coloured the whole of our lives.

For an hour, on three evenings of the week, he took us. In that hour we did nothing at all, but sat staring, arms folded, eyes straight ahead, while he walked up and down, whistling under his breath a tune from his army days, and waiting, watching for a chance to pounce.

A boy winked across to another.

A little boy smiled, taut with nerves.

'Come out!'

Then, with closed fist – smash!

The boy reeled, staggered, but came up again – to attention. Smash!

'What're you crying for, eh?' Another fist.

'Nothing, sir!' 'Nothing, sir! I'm – not – not crying, sir!' With the tears streaming down his face.

'Put that face straight!' Smash! And another, and yet another, till the boy's face was, somehow, straightened.

I GO TO SCHOOL

'Now keep it straight.'

'Yes, sir,' managing somehow to stand upright before the bully. 'Yes, sir. I am, sir. I'm not crying, sir. Not now, sir!'

Little boys with blinding tears running down their cheeks.

The Labour Master was not allowed to use the cane. Only the Schoolmaster did that.

'Charlie,' he'd say, 'put that boy on your back.'

And Charlie, the biggest boy in the school, bent over, pulled the boy up over his back, and crossing his arms on his chest, gripped the boy's hands and held him secure.

Then came the cane, a length of drain cane. One. Two. Three. Four. Never more than four. More were not needed.

Afterwards, white as a sheet, the delinquent was stood in a corner. Often there'd be a crash, and the boy was down in a faint. Another boy threw water over him to bring him round. That was all; and that was all the attention he attracted.

I saw and I suffered so much in that school that I have never lifted a hand against my own children.

Four different times I went there, and three times I was discharged for good conduct, sent home, cured. But I wasn't cured. As soon as I could, I was back to the brickfield, bird-snaring and catching, and rose-selling, and taking pleasure in the green land again.

But every time the School Board Man was after me, caught me in the end, and back I had to go.

Every time I was taken back I was made doorboy, except the last.

Then the Schoolmaster said to me, 'No sweets for *you* this time, Curtis, nothing but the sours.'

Even then the new doorboy fell ill, and he had to come to me. 'You'd better do it after all!' he said. They trusted me, you see. Partly perhaps because of that prize that had followed me to the school, but mostly because they wanted a boy they could rely upon to use his wits.

We had to use them. Being doorboy made life almost tolerable.

I was always there when parents came to see their boys.

A ring. I'd hurry to the door and open it.

'Good morning, ma'm.'

'Good morning, I want to see my Willie.'

'Yes, m'm. Come inside and wait a minute, m'm.'

I had to go through two big halls, and come back through them, with Willie. All the way back I was working on him.

'Now, Willie, you won't forget my share? You'll remember me; remember, half for me, Willie, eh? I'm taking you to your mother now. She's waiting for you. You won't forget now, Willie?'

And after a quarter of an hour, I had to take him back, across those two big halls.

'An orange for me, remember, Willie, you promised. And half your pocket money, don't forget.'

And poor little Willie, all of atremble with the parting, and with the tears running down his face, never knew one-half the treasure he was parting with.

The last time I went to school I had only twelve weeks to do to reach the leaving age.

The day before I came to fourteen, I asked to see the Schoolmaster as he came in. 'Please, sir,' I said, 'can I get my clothes, and go home tomorrow?'

'Home? Home? Why, you're only just here!'

'But sir, I'm fourteen tomorrow.'

'You're nothing of the sort. You've twelve months to do here. You're only thirteen.'

My heart stopped. Twelve months to do! It worried me so, I couldn't sleep but lay awake all night. For I couldn't be certain that I was fourteen.

Next morning at eight o'clock I was back at my old job – on the door.

The Schoolmaster came down. Without a word he went to the safe and got out my warrant. He looked at it, and then at me.

'Curtis,' he said, 'get your clothes out. You're going home this afternoon.'

I'd finished school, having fared better than many. I'd learned to read and to write. I'd even had my hand put to a trade, had I a wish to follow it, for in the workshop I had made a pair of button-up boots to take home. But most important of all, I'd learned to look after myself.

Before I left I was given a pair of knee breeches with pearl buttons down the side at the knee, and a good pair of thick socks. I never thought to wonder how they came to be left.

From the Bank, where everybody's money was kept, I drew twenty-two shillings and sixpence. No, not all from boys. Often their parents gave me something before they left, and of course my own parents had given me some.

I was fourteen. Four times I had been in school—for truanting. One year and ten months of schooling, one year and two months of freedom. I was fourteen; finished with school, such as I had known it.

I went straight back to the wild life.

Freedom Again

I WAS free to run wild a little longer. You may think it strange, perhaps, when fourteen was the age at which most boys set out to look for work. Any work. Good jobs were hard to find: the boys I knew took any employment that would bring in a few shillings a week. They went into jobs that had no future. They delivered groceries, carrying weights beyond their strength. They swung in the open backs of horse vans, saving themselves every few minutes from disaster by the rope that dangled from the roof, and parting with cheek and advice to all and sundry. Others went with the baker on his rounds, and carried the heavy basket of sweet-smelling bread on aching arms. They staggered on wintry days with the milkman, carrying a metal can of half-frozen milk from which to fill the cans that stood on doorsteps. They swept the floors and polished the counters and cleaned the windows and fronts of shops; they stood in the dark evenings, long after all the customers had gone home, with tired faces, weighing out the goods for the next day's sale. And as soon as they were no longer boys, but came of age and asked for a rise, they were out of a job.

Sooner or later, it seemed, I must join them, for I had had no education to fit me for much else. But I was allowed my freedom. Ours was an easy-going family; so long as there was food in the house and money for the rent, we were content. People today, when everyone clamours for higher and higher wages, without seeing that in the end they will be no better off, have no idea how little money, as money, meant to those in our station. Its only value was as food and clothing. So I was free for a while, and in me grew the resentment of the wild against the trap, the cage of shop or factory. I would escape, and perfect, instead, the poacher's art, the skills of trap and snare and shooting. I knew by upbringing that life could be lived and enjoyed richly, if the wide fields were my second home and butcher and fishmonger, yes, and often bed, too.

I went alone into the fields, watching and learning the habits of beast and bird: song and flight, and where the birds dropped down to feed, and where they went to drink, and where to roost. I saw the hawfinch fly to the hedgetree with a love-offering of a leaf held in his beak: I turned the stones in winter to discover the hard seeds he sought there, that I might use that knowledge in his taking.

I watched the rabbit shake the dew from his feet in the silver morning, and saw in the grass the prints where his feet had fallen in his exit from the thicket. I took off my shoes and went barefoot, not in the streets as so many of us did, but barefoot through the dew-chill grass, and never took cold. I crept along the hedge and saw the sun come red and vast through the stems, felt its sudden warmth, saw my shadow run away down before me, the whole length of the field, and the lark spring from that field with bursting throat. And, being a boy, I had with me always my catapult and my traps, for a boy sees nothing cruel in killing and in eating what he has taken delight in watching, for the boy is a hunter, learning through watching to hunt the better.

I went again to the brickfield to catch birds, for the owl I found was alive, and hungry still.

Other boys were soon eager to join me, for the brickfield was a no-man's-land of adventure. We caught birds, and we sold their bodies, and when there were too many for the owl, we brought them back again to the brickfield and cooked them and ate them ourselves.

We took off their heads, unless the trap had done that for us, then we plucked and gutted their soft carcases, only leaving in the little heart to be a dainty. Sparrows and starlings;

little enough on each for growing boys: half an ounce of meat on a sparrow, an ounce perhaps on a starling.

Now that I was back on the brickfield, it was easy to fall into the old ways, of going down to the soup kitchen for a free meal, of begging and scrounging and scrumping.

There is an art in scrumping; it lies in taking enough to make being caught worthwhile, and then to escape after all.

I went home one day, to make preparations for getting apples and pears. Life seemed unchanged. 'Mother,' I said, 'I want needle and cotton please, and an old skirt.' All easy enough to find in our house, and I knew almost as well as Mother how to use a needle after the school I'd been to.

I took off my jacket, and from the skirt I made a big pocket, sewing it into the back of the jacket, from collar to bottom, and from side to side. I put on the jacket, called to Mother that I was off for a few apples, and set out. There was only one thing bothering me. When I was up a tree, I liked to have pockets that I could cram full, to be emptied when I climbed down. My trousers had no pockets. Mother had found putting them in too difficult, and had left them out. But luck was in my way, for in the street I met one of my brothers wearing a pair of father's trousers, cut down, but complete with pockets. We exchanged trousers there and then, in the street.

The orchard was full of summer, with grasses tall enough to hide me lying down. I took off my jacket and laid it hidden under a tree. I climbed among the branches. I filled my pockets; came down again and filled my jacket at the back. After a time I began to have doubts as to whether I should be able to carry home all that load. But it wasn't till I was ready to come home that I found my real mistake. So swollen was the coat with apples and pears, I couldn't get my arm into the second sleeve!

I usually went alone on these expeditions. By myself I could escape detection, or at least escape; and my brothers had their own amusements, their own troubles.

Sometimes my sister Alice would come. One day Mother had asked her to run out and buy some firewood, a farthing a bundle it was. I ran out after Alice. 'No need to waste a penny,' I said, 'we can have that. I know where there's some

FREEDOM AGAIN

firewood.' I did. There was a good paling loose in a fence, it only wanted knocking out. We armed ourselves with the hammer and set off.

But Alice's tooth was all I knocked out. I took a mighty swipe and the hammer slipped out of my grasp and caught Alice in the face. She forgave me, and would still come with me – when I would let her.

There came another time when Mother ran out of fuel – no fire, and no coal to make one with.

'Alice,' I said, 'I know where there's some heaps of coal.' Without a word to Mother, we slipped out of the room, got hold of two shopping bags, and set off for the brickfield.

There, stood two mounds of coal, unfortunately well in sight of passers-by.

'You keep watch,' I whispered, 'and give a call if you're seen.'

The coal was small, it took some time to fill the bags.

I was just finishing the second, when there was a shout. I looked up. Alice had vanished. She had been waiting by a big circular pit where lime and clay were mixed for the making of white bricks. We had often watched the work there, walking round with the horse as it stirred the mixture with a heavy flange attached to a pole. Alice was in the pit. Luckily it wasn't full, but poor Alice was white from shoulders down, and half frozen.

We hurried off home. As we were standing at the door, wondering what tale to tell, Mother opened the door and saw us, a study in black and white. 'Wherever have you two been?' she cried. 'You'll get yourselves locked up. And what's that you've got – coal?' She hurried us in, and very warm and bright was the fire she made, with Alice sitting by it, thawing out.

Spring came. The grasses bent in long waves to the wind. The warm breath brought the swallows. The trees moved with soft whisper of sound. The old restlessness moved in me again like a fever. I began to stay more and more away from home.

Some days I begged. I waited outside the factory gates as the men came from work, and begged for bread – sandwiches left or saved for me from the midday lunch. I had special clients too, who made arrangements to meet me the next day and had a piece of cake ready for me.

To make money, I sold watercress. I went down to the Edmonton sewage farm, and bought what was known as a hand of cress – a shilling's worth. I bundled it up with bast, hawked it round the streets, and could sell my shilling's worth for half a crown.

On Sundays men used to take their whippets to the Marshes and train them for rabbit coursing. I'd go along too. Between times I searched around the rifle butts, where I could pick up flattened bullets – we could get a halfpenny a pound for lead.

Then during the week two of us would get a sack or an old shopping bag, and collect rags and bones, going round the backs of the houses and sorting out what we wanted, for both rags and bones were saleable. Sometimes a policeman would stop us, wanting to know what we had in the bag, but he didn't stop our sales.

And when the dusty day was gone, and night came from the ends of streets and gathered in alley-ways, I would count over my money; and if I had enough food and could find the coppers to spare, I would go just as I had done in the old days, to see a play at the Gaff or at the Tottenham Palace, both the same price, twopence in the gods. When I did turn up at home nobody minded, or said I should be within doors. Boys of our generation and class learned to stand on their feet, and to care for themselves. Our lives we largely carved out for ourselves. And as our lives were our own, so were our amusements, though not necessarily the better for that.

We played in the streets, whip-tops for the girls, peg-top, for the boys. We made 'hummers' by removing the peg from the top, pushing a little horse-dropping into the hole, and replacing the peg. We made our 'bangers': a long door key with the heads of matches stuffed into the hollow shaft to be the explosive, and a big nail to be the trigger. We pushed the nail into the key, tied the ends of a piece of string to each, and swung the head of the nail against the wall of somebody's house. We left other bangers on the railway lines to be set off by passing trains. On the lines too, we made rough penknife blades, leaving a three-inch nail to be flattened by the wheels. They worked too, when we had put them into a wooden handle and sharpened them. They trimmed the handles for our catapults.

We had other amusements. We tied long strings to a series of knockers on front doors, and hid away, and annoyed the neighbours by pulling on the string and bringing them bewildered to the door. We'd get a trouser button, tie it to a piece of cotton, and with a pin, hang it above a window. At every breath of air, the button tap-tapped on the window, and we'd hide opposite to see a puzzled face come again and again to the glass to see who or what was tapping.

Other boys, better off, had their hoops of iron, and ran miles round the evening streets with the hoop ringing musically beside them. Others, on roller skates, swept from side to side of the road, under the bellies of passing horses. Every passing van was a chariot for us to ride free, having a 'whippy' at the back. Days were leisured and yet full. Days you will never know.

Morning began with the ringing metallic clatter and crunch of the milk-float over the stones of the road, bright with dew. 'Milk, Milk-o-oho!' the milkman cried, his voice echoing down the street, vying with other milkmen in neighbouring streets, and growing louder as he came, till below the window there sounded his strong step and the clatter of the milk-can. There was no such thing then as a milk-bottle of glass, every customer had her own can, and scoured it spotless. Those were the days when dairies, instead of vying with the grocer, sold pots of cream, little brown glazed jugs of cream – for sixpence: and butter was plentiful and cheap.

When the milk-float was on its round for the second time, for the milkman called twice a day, the baker's van was on the rounds too, breathing the warm reek of bread.

The oilman called regularly with his strong cart and big horse. The butcher delivered the joint, calling at the houses in the better part of the town in his trap with high-stepping horse. The coalman delivered good coal and cheap, and brought it cheerfully to you without thought of tip. The cats-meat man pushed strong brown meat strung on a skewer through the letter-box of every house where he saw a pet. The muffin man, his wares in a tray on his head, walked slowly, and turned to watch for opening doors, and rang his hand-bell to announce his coming. The knife-grinder pushed his barrow along interminable streets, sharpening knives and scissors and shears for a few pence a time. Newsboys ran through the streets crying the news of the day, and the names of the papers they carried.

Towards dusk, when the summer heats had dried the metalled roads to a desert of dust, the water cart would creep up the edge of the street, and lay the dust with a summer sweetness, while children ran in and out of the curving streams that jetted from the rear of the cart.

And in the long dusks, when fathers sat in shirt sleeves in search of coolness, and mothers talked at street doors with neighbours, wailing down the streets would come the lament of the begging street singers, with their travesty of hymns and sentimental songs: 'Abide with me' and 'Underneath the gaslamp's glitter'. With lynx eyes they saw every watching face, every hand about to open a window to throw a coin. Sometimes would come a real musician, playing with double-stopping the well-known airs from the operas, filling the street with a strange beauty of sound. Then his cap would be busy, and for every coin he had a gracious bow. We would guess at how they came to be here, and who they might be – musicians unable to find enough work to make a living, or who perhaps had lost a job through drink, for drunkenness was a common failing and the sight of man or woman fighting drunk, being taken to the police station, was familiar to us. Those were the days when we could buy five different comics for one penny; and we read a fearsome paper called the *Bloody Budget*, a picture paper with all the horrifying details of the murders of the week. We read other news in the paper wrapped round mother's fish – fresh herrings, eight for fourpence, and all good fish. Food was plentiful, living was cheap: only money itself was scarce.

During my fifteenth year, I made a small fortune in one week, though it had taken me many weeks to be able to earn it. I had always been interested in tap-dancing: the urge to rhythm was in my feet as it was in my hands. While the rest were playing with their whip-tops, I was in a corner practising steps with a chosen friend or two. Song after song we learned to tap-dance to, thirty-four different sets of steps: and old pensioner though I now am, I can do them still, for once the balance and control are learnt, they can never be lost.

I had a special friend as keen on the dancing as I was myself and far better at it. This was Marci the Italian ice-cream vendor, and often I wandered with him on his rounds, and he taught me, in the long interludes when nobody wanted a glass of ice-cream, to dance the steps he knew.

One day when we were dancing, Mr. Moss the manager of the Gaff chanced to come along, saw us, and stopped to watch.

'I'll give you boys a chance one of these days, on the stage,' he promised. We practised now, every spare minute we could find, and Mr. Moss was as good as his word. A week or two later we were invited to show our skill – but separately, this time.

Marci went first on to the stage, and danced to music, tapping out the tune with his feet, and I felt I could never beat it. Then it was my turn. All the music I asked for was the tapping of my own feet – for this was what we had learnt to do in the streets, marking the steps with our slate pencils on to slates, and practising their rhythm.

I was the winner. I had beaten the man who taught me. The prize was a windfall for any boy – a week's contract to appear at the Gaff, and at the end of the week, five pounds in cash. I spent some of it straight away. I went up to Petticoat Lane and fitted myself out with clothes. Thirty-two shillings I spent, and the rest I took home.

Now I found other little jobs to do, but they led nowhere, and they did not last, so that the old indolent way of life asserted itself, till Father insisted that I find employment.

I Go to Work

I found myself where I had vowed never to be – inside a factory, a sweet factory. Before long I was actually making sweets: the sherbet dabs that were sold in the shops for a farthing each. First I took the wooden mould that was to hold the dabs, and pressed it into a box of starch to stop the toffee from sticking. There were hollows in the mould, and next I dropped a spoonful of toffee into each; waited till they were set, then lifted them out. Then they went into their paper bag with the sherbet; and very popular they were among school-children, together with other 'sweets' seldom seen today: locust beans and fairy flakes and tiger nuts.

A big tub of treacle stood in the room. When dinner hour came and we all trooped out for a breath of fresh air and something to eat, I would linger behind till all had gone, then down into the tub I'd reach and gulp a hasty mouthful, for like most boys, my tooth was sweet. It was only afterwards that I sometimes suffered – when I found that treacle did not go well with a ha'porth of fried fish and a ha'porth of chip potatoes.

There was another tub in the corner of the room – stood by the door so that we could give it a handy stir as we passed. It needed stirring. It contained the mixture for making the licorice that was so popular and so cheap. What a mixture it was! Nothing was wasted that might go into it. The sweepings from the benches with all the remnants of the ingredients that had been in use, mingled with straw from the packing cases, and sweepings from the floor, yes, and mouse dirts and even mice. I've seen a whole litter of baby mice go in, little hairless creatures still pink. No wonder it was due to be stirred every time we passed, and no wonder that licorice was cheap. But then, as I have said, everything was cheap, including labour. The money I received from the sherbet mills would be scorned by any boy today, and yet it was good money. Six and tenpence a week I earned, paid in halfpence and farthings. We used to declare it must be the takings from the sale of licorice and sherbet dabs. I'd take it home, and empty the lot into Mother's coarse apron. She seldom counted it straight away, and by the time she did some of us had helped ourselves to pocket money. She never grumbled; but once she had counted it out and stood my wages in little piles along the dresser shelf, she knew it was safe.

Had I only known it, the girl I was to marry years after was working there in the factory with me. Perhaps I didn't stay long enough to find out, for though the time was all too long for me, in the end I found myself on the streets again.

I made friends with a flower seller: a man poor as we were, one of many who tramped the streets carrying a basket of plants and flowers, hawking them from door to door, making a few coppers. I used to help him, for while he had his own set route, I could nip up the side streets and little entries and reach people he would never meet. Lilies-of-the-valley were one of my best lines, and I'd hold a few in each hand, after I'd knocked, and use the charm I had found so effective at the Truant School. The money we earned was not ours, of course, it must go back to the man who owned both basket and flowers. One day, just before Derby Day, my friend said, 'We won't take the money back tonight, I'll make it all right when I go again. Let's go to the Derby.' And he put the basket over a wall. I was ready for any adventure, and when he assured me that we would get lifts on the way to help us out, I agreed.

On the eve of the Derby we arrived. We had a meal at a coffee-stall, something hot to keep us warm so that we should be able to sleep, for it was raining hard. We crept under the Grandstand, and huddled together trying to keep warm. We must have slept, for in the morning something was lying near me on the ground – a parcel I hadn't seen the night before, and one that is a mystery to me today. In it was a man's coat, fur-lined, and with fur collar. I had no idea whose it was, but it was there beside me, so I put it on and felt like the King of England.

'My,' said the flower seller, 'you look just like a jockey. Tell you what, we'll buy some race cards and you can go among the crowd and sell them.' We did. We bought a hundred cards at threepence each, and sold them for double.

By the time of the race we had good viewing points at the side of the Course.

I got up on the rails to see better. Suddenly there was a great shout, 'They're off!' In my excitement I tumbled off the rails on to the Course. I heard the coming thunder of the hoofs. In a moment I should be trampled underfoot. In desperation I leaped up at the rails, and flung my arms round the neck of an old gentleman. The thunder grew in my ears.

It roared past me mingled with the roar of the crowd. I could smell leather and horses, and hear the voice of a jockey; then they were gone, and there was commotion all around. The old gentleman was shouting that I had tried to steal his watch and chain, and calling on those near by to fetch a policeman. But they could see his watch safely there, untouched, and more than one had seen me tumble. In the end he let me go, and very glad I was to be off and get safely home, with the coat that had turned up so mysteriously.

Mother listened to my story, looked at the coat and took it round to the pawnbroker's. I shall never forget that Derby. It was memorable in another way too, for in that year King Edward the Seventh won the race, with his horse Minoru.

And so my days went by, with work and the lack of it, and odd things happening that today seem almost incredible to me.

It was strange how jobs would turn up. One evening I was out, with nothing much to do. A man asked me if I would help him catch his chickens which had broken out and given him a hard hour trying to get them back. I enjoyed the next half-hour, for anything to do with bird or animal gave me pleasure.

When they were safely housed he asked who I was, and where I lived, and then he said, 'Would you like a job with me?' It turned out he was a foreman at the Gothic Engineering Works in Edmonton. I started the next week: shaping the ends of little spindles, a thousand in a week. Sometimes when he saw that I would never get through them in time, he would switch me to burring over guides for gas-meters, an easy job that enabled me to take home my money at the end of the week – ten shillings in a week, more than I had ever earned before, and good money for a boy with no training. These tasks I enjoyed, for they were bringing skill to my hands that were always for the making of things. They were the very beginnings of the training I was later to get, and that gave me the skill for the making of nets, and the 'needles' that we used for them, as well as the fashioning of traps and snares and devices for bird catching.

Then Father got me a different job. He was now at Gamages, still working as a scaffolder. Gamages had suffered

a great fire, and everywhere there were salvaged goods.
Father bought some old shoes, second-hand, at a penny or
twopence a pair. We would each turn up in a pair in the
morning, then change out of sight into a new undamaged pair.
Then we'd walk about in the mortar and rubble till the newness
had gone; and they were ours. We found other salvaged goods.
We would go into the lavatory and put on a new shirt, and
another on top of it, and another on top of that if we could
manage it, and go home fatter than we came. One day we
found a parcel marked 'Tablecloths' and carried that all the
way home – only to find they were paper ones.

Dishonest? Yes, I suppose it was dishonest, yet somehow
we didn't feel we were hurting Gamages but only those who
later would obtain the salvage goods for not much more than
we were giving.

We used to cycle to work. I had a lady's cycle, one with
drop handlebars, not easy to control. One morning as I was
going, alone, I saw a horse almost on top of me. I swung round
it and went into the cart instead. When I had picked myself
up, I saw the bicycle was useless, the front wheel badly buckled.

I arrived for work about an hour late. As I went in, Mr. Gamage
was standing there. He gave me a quick look. 'You work here?'

'Yes, sir.'

'What's the matter?' I told him of the accident. Then he
wanted to know who I was, and when I'd told him, he asked me
to wait. He took a card from his vest pocket, and scribbled a
note upon it. 'There, take this up into the bicycle room,' he
said. I went up and showed the card.

The assistant gave it one glance. 'Here you are, son,' he said,
'pick one for yourself.' A free bicycle! I took a Raleigh.

The time came at last when Father and I fell out. I decided
to leave home. It was to be years before I returned to the
fields and the folk I loved so well.

A man at work had been telling of the job he had been
engaged upon, farther north, in Manchester.

I Leave Home

I decided I would try for Manchester.
Work in the North, I found, was not easy to obtain; I

must take anything that offered or starve. There began a time of dreary trudging around, of getting jobs that did not last, of finding work uncongenial to my taste: days and months when all I longed for, the free woods and the fields, seemed gone for ever. Yet I kept the urge within me, the need to get out into the countryside that I understood, and where, it seemed, I could always make life a little easier – not by working on the land, for which I had had no training, but living off the land.

I ended up in a factory once more; the great works of the Fine Spinners' Association in Hulme. I had never seen so many women and girls at work together before. My experience at the Gothic Works had helped me to get in as fitter's mate. I would never be rich, but at least I could pay for my board and lodging. Lodgings I had found in Hood Street, a shilling a night. We had our meals in one dining room. There I met three coloured men, each with a caste mark on his forehead. They were, I understood, survivors from a wreck, and we were soon good friends, sharing all that came in. They would draw up to table, empty their pockets on to a plate, decide how much was to be spent, and send out the youngest to make the purchase: any money that remained was shared out equally. Before long their number was increased to four. One day they came across another man with the same mark upon his forehead. He was playing a guitar outside a public house. They smashed the guitar as unworthy of him, and took him home to become one of themselves.

I was still working at the mills, with work not hard, and the money sufficient, but it was to end abruptly.

The foreman had sent me up one day with a bucket of soapy water to pour on to a hot bearing. High above the ground, I looked around in awe at all the white rope belts that drove the machinery throughout the building – more than thirty belts of rope.

As I looked, one snapped. I saw it catch the foreman where he stood on his platform. Horrified, I watched it hurl him to the ground, and heard his cry as he was dashed to the floor. He was dead when they picked him up. This, I thought, is factory life: these, are the terrible things that can catch you within-doors.

I felt I could never settle; and I left at the end of the week.

My search began all over again. I found work at last with an engineeering firm, and could have had regular employment with them. The First World War had started, and the firm wanted men to sign on 'for the duration' as we came to say, but inside me was still the longing for the out-of-doors that seemed now farther away than ever. When they pressed me to sign, I left. I felt like an animal that has just escaped the trap.

But times grew harder. I tried my hand at any job that offered reasonable hope. I went tyre-stripping, working with coloured people whose hands seemed made of tough leather. My own were soft, and before long they too were stripped. In despair I went to a chemist, and asked him to help me. The only thing he had he said, was tannin. I tried it. My hands were soon as dark as some of those with whom I worked, but the skin hardened, and I was able to carry on my work. Work? It was slave labour – three-farthings for stripping a heavy tyre completely. I could see that unless I did something more, I should never be able to throw off the yoke that held me.

I was doing more. In the evenings I was helping an old Jew with his clock- and watch-mending. Unlikely though it may sound, through that work I began to feel my way towards salvation and freedom. My employer found that I had a readiness in my fingers, and skill already growing in them. He started by giving me an alarm clock to take down, clean and reassemble. He was pleased with the job. He gave me other clocks, and watches. Then I found that he could mend other things as well, sewing machines included. He taught me what he knew of those, and especially how most of their troubles were of their owner's making, and easily put right with a little knowledge and skill, and the right tools.

I walked back one evening to my lodgings, with the wind blowing the scent of green grass in my thoughts. I knew how I would do it: how I would be free again. Freedom tugged at my sleeve: I could smell rabbit cooking, for suppers yet to be. I worked harder, putting by in my memory of head and finger all the Jew could teach me. I put money aside, and the day came when I had enough to buy myself a kit of tools. With them I bought a can of engine oil, thinned it down with paraffin and put it up into little bottles: my stock of lubricating oil for sale to customers.

I Find Freedom

There came the morning when I took the road. I was free at last. I was a travelling repairer. Five shillings I would charge, for cleaning and oiling, and putting the tensions right.

I met with suspicion. This was Derbyshire, and I was a Londoner, a Cockney to them, and therefore rogue and thief.

But I made a start, and from that start grew a steady round of custom.

I knocked at a door in a little town.

'Good morning, ma'am.' (And how well I knew just how to say that, after being door-boy at school!) 'Good morning, ma'am. I call from the sewing machine repair department. Is there anything you require this morning?'

There was. I was invited in to look at the machine. And all the time the woman hovered round in obvious agitation and distress. It seemed she daren't leave me. Then I found out why. In one of the drawers of the machine she had hidden her money.

'Madam,' I said, without turning round, 'will you please take this money?' I could feel her relief – and from that moment we were friends. She sent me on to friends of hers, and I was set fair.

Of course, there were difficulties with machines I had never seen before, but after a month or so I felt I could tackle any. I had cleaned family machines made by Jones, many and many a Singer, and an old machine in the shape of a lion. It was a bit rusty, and there were one or two pieces I had to replace, but when I had seen to these trifles, it worked as well as new. Later it was put up for auction, for anything patriotic caught the popular fancy, and the British Lion Sewing Machine fetched a good sum for the Red Cross.

There was a Robert How machine I had to attend to, and for which I was paid no money. It was in a queer household, a mother with three daughters, all grown up, and every one of them a simple. They covered me with confusion, sitting giggling at my work. I was glad to be away, and never called again: yet they had paid me handsomely, with a silver tea-pot they insisted on my having.

I think the hardest machine I had to tackle was one with a name that sounded German, a Frister and Rossman. I managed it, but I doubt if in that part of the country they would have found another man to touch it, with the feeling there was against the 'Huns'.

From town and village I found time to go into the country lanes, and took a toll, though a light one as yet. There were rabbits in plenty. Sometimes a farmer gave me permission to take from his fields, and when he did not, I controlled his rabbits for him.

A morning walk would show me where to come again. Before dusk my snare was in position, and there was rabbit next day. I needed no expensive gear. I could get a supper with little more trouble than it took to cover the holes – except one. There had come on to the market a substance new to me, calcium carbide, used for cycle lamps. I would push a few lumps of it into the hole left open, wet them, and block up the hole with turf sods, leaving just a small hole for me to blow through when the gas was given off. Then the rabbits bolted, unless they were overcome in the tunnel. That didn't mean a rabbit lost. I'd get a length of barbed wire, push it into the hole till bunny was reached, twist it in his fur, and draw him out. If there was no wire, then a nice brier stem would do, or even a hawthorn branch.

Even calcium carbide was not essential. A winter warmer would do, a thing unheard of nowadays, yet every schoolboy had one when I was young. It was simply a tin with holes punched in for ventilation, and filled with smouldering rag. It kept hands and pocket beautifully warm. For rabbiting all that was needed was a little flowers of sulphur dusted on to the burning rag: the fumes would bring out any rabbit.

One day I was invited to a rabbit shoot – but not to do the shooting.

I was sitting in the hedge, looking at a likely place for to-morrow's supper. Along the road came an old woman, driving a cow. She stopped and got into conversation. Eight miles she had taken the cow, to be bulled, and now she had had to collect her and walk back with her. Thirteen fine sons she had, she said, and only two not away fighting the Kaiser. One she had lost. 'Ah,' she said, 'the terrible slaughter at the Darbyelles. If I had my way, I'd hang t'old Kaiser ont' telegrams.'

I walked a mile or so with her, and then she said I might as well finish the way and have a meal with them. Over dinner we fell to talking of the land and country matters, and I was given freedom of the farmland to take what I wanted for as long as I was in the neighbourhood. 'There's a big shoot, if you'd like to come along next week,' the farmer told me. 'There'll be guns from miles around.'

I was there. Someone called for a volunteer to handle the ferrets, and I said I'd do it.

I had never seen so many rabbits run before: nor so much skilful shooting. But of course there was one 'Willie' as there seems to be in every shooting party – somebody with plenty of cartridges, a good gun, and no idea of how to use it. He spoiled many another's chance, and the rabbits escaped. They ran swiftly to the stone walls, with others that had bolted, and disappeared within. Once they were in, I put the ferrets in after. They worked the walls as the wild stoat does, running through the hidden passages of the wall, and coming to peer out with weak eyes every dozen yards or so, as if to see how things were going, or perhaps to take bearings.

Things went well. Some of the guns had lined up along the wall; the rabbits ran out into a blaze of fire.

When all was over, and the rabbits gathered up, they filled the two-wheeled cart that had been standing all day in readiness. For once there was no need for me to poach. There were thank-you's for my handling of the ferrets – obviously a thing I was used to. I didn't tell them that I had only handled them once or twice in my life, and that with Father, poaching

Another day I was not far from Bugsworth. I came upon a large house, deserted. I walked in through the open gates, and strolled about the grounds, looking with interest at plants and trees new to me. I could enjoy life, I thought, in such a place, with the wild enclosed for me, up to my very doors. Then I saw that the house was open, with the doors standing wide. I went in.

Before long I was aware of an odour: a stench of something dead and decaying. A murder, I thought, and the body lying here undiscovered. I followed the smell, up the stairs, and to the very room. I pushed the door suddenly open. I have never seen such a sight. Rabbits guts: dozens, scores, hundreds, of entrails, and all decomposing. I shut the door, glad to get away and out into the fresh air. This was the work of a gang of poachers, and here they had come, to the seclusion of this deserted mansion, to strip their booty.

I Join the Army

Time passed. The war dragged on: the war that was to be over in a few months. I joined up.

I went to Felixstowe; and well I remember some of my training days, along the shingle beaches where the stones run for miles in high ridges, and marching is a fatigue in itself.

At night, came the canteen and the marquee. A few of us had a corner to ourselves one night, with a Crown and Anchor board. My luck was in; do what I could it seemed impossible for me to lose. At the end of play I had more pounds than I liked to carry about with me, and more than were safe to carry. The corporal who had been playing with us came to me and said, 'Here, boy, shove your Bradbury's into that, and then put it round your waist -- and keep it there.' He gave me a blow belt – the men used to make them and decorate them themselves. I put the money into an opening, blew it around the body of the belt, and put on the belt. It was just as well I did.

A night or two later, we had been having a little celebration at my expense, and we came back with a few drinks too many.

I went to my tent and lay down. I woke up, in hospital.

'What am I in here for, Nurse?' I asked.

The doctor came over. 'Ah, so we're better,' he said smiling. 'Somebody hit you on the head with a tent mallet, Curtis.'

A terrible fear came over me. 'Did they get my money, sir?'

'They tried their best, but it's all safely put by for you.'

I heard the rest of the story later. It seems that the corporal was disturbed from sleep by something – the mallet I expect. He opened his eyes, and saw a hand fumbling about my body.

He leaped up, and jabbed his bayonet through the wall of the tent. Sure enough, a man reported sick with a cut wrist; he was in hospital too.

A week they kept me. As soon as I was out, I went straight into town and spent the money, the whole lot, in presents, cutlery and so forth, and sent them home to Mother. I had nothing left to rob.

Later they called for volunteers to go to Scotland to help with the building of airfields. I went. And there, for the first time in my life, I met true Highlanders, men who had never seen a cinema in their lives, men with hair on their chests thick as a mat and appetites that made you feel afraid. They would eat enough porridge at one sitting to last me for a week. They could work on it, and they did so, cheerfully, with the good temper of most strong men. 'Jock', when some particularly heavy or awkward piece of rock wanted shifting, 'Jock, here's one you'll not move. You'll not shift that!' But Jock could, and did; and never once took offence at being imposed upon.

As the weeks slipped away, it became evident that the blow on my head had done more damage than was thought. I was put on Reserve.

And at long last, I found myself home again, with Father and Mother, and my sister Tilly gone out now to work. Sometimes she would bring home her friend from work, and it was not long before she and I had struck up a friendship, one that was to last all our lives, for she was to become my wife, and share all the hazards, and the joys, of the poaching life.

Strangely now that I was with Father again, it seemed that the years from home had never been. I began shooting again with him. I heard of a man who had two guns for sale, cheap. I made arrangements to meet him with the guns, on the allotments where we sometimes shot. I took with me my brother Bill, also on the look-out for a gun. One was an underlever, and the other a lightweight gun, a lady's model by Haste and White, a double-barrelled twelve. They were cheap, as we had heard. We decided to have a shot or two. Bill decided on the underlever, and paid £5 down for it.

I turned to the man still holding the other gun. 'I'll throw a jam-jar into the air,' I said, 'and you shoot it.' The man went pale. 'No, no, no, not today, I couldn't shoot today, you try!'

I emptied the left barrel, shattered the jar, and bought the gun. That was a Saturday. On the Monday next, Bill didn't go to work, but came with me instead, on to the marshlands. It came on to rain, and for two hours we had the Marshes to ourselves. At the end of that time I still did not know what was wrong with the gun I had bought, I only knew that every kill had been made with the left barrel. I could see nothing amiss. So now I took it in my hands, looked away out into the streaming rain, and passed the barrel slowly through my hand, feeling with blind delicate finger-tip for knock or dent invisible to the eye. I could find nothing. We stood up to wait for the rain to stop. We waited till we could see it was hopeless.

'Come on,' I said to Bill, 'let's take what we've got and get home out of the wet.' We passed through the allotments, with myself feeling very bitter to think that I had been deceived over a gun.

Overhead the starlings were blowing on the wind, going over the grey sky in little flocks to their London roosting grounds.

'I'll have one last try,' I said, swung round, and emptied the right barrel into the starlings. The gun exploded in my hand.

In blind anger I picked up the pieces. 'I'll see you later, Bill!' I called, and set off straightway for the man who had sold me the gun.

I knocked. The door half opened.

'Good evening,' I began, 'I've come . . .'

'Something's happened to the gun,' he interrupted. 'Oh, I knew it would, I knew it would. Are you hurt?'

'No, but wait till you've seen the gun.'

'Come in, come in,' he said in scarcely more than a whisper, and shut the door to, behind me.

Then he told me the story of how, some months previously, he had shot a man by accident with that very gun, of how all this time he had been keeping the man's family whilst he recovered in hospital. 'I knew something dreadful would happen with it,' he said. 'I ought never to have sold it.'

He insisted on refunding fifty shillings of the purchase money. 'Now what will you do?' he asked.

'Leave the gun with me, I may be able to do something with it,' I said.

I took it home and had a good look at it. The damage I saw was less extensive than I had feared. I had no intention of using it again, but I could patch it up. I set to work with white solder, mended the breaks, burnished it all over so that nothing showed and you could not have told there had ever been anything wrong. I would get rid of it, I thought. I took it round to the pawnshop, and realised four pounds on it. 'Good-bye!' I said to it in my heart, for I never wanted to handle it again.

Yet it turned up some fourteen months later. One evening just as duck time was closing in the sky, my brother Bill hurried by with a friend.

'Hullo, where are you off?'

'Going to try out a gun. Joe here's just bought it from the pawnshop.'

I gave it one look. 'Bill,' I cried, 'don't you use that gun. Don't you remember? – it's mine!'

Joe looked at me as if I were daft, and hurried Bill away.

When they got to the fields, they did at least take the precaution of tying a string to the trigger.

And when they fired, the right breech opened up half an inch, and locked the cartridge in the left – a complete loss.

Next morning they were back at the pawnbroker's. He would have nothing to do with it. He had taken it in good faith, he said, and that was that. The worst day's work I ever did with a gun; not that I had ever thought that anyone I knew would buy it.

I Get Married

All this time I was courting, and going shooting with Father whenever the chance came.

Alongside the allotments where we shot ran farmfields. Sheep offal and fish had been spread over them for enriching th grouend. The smell was unbelievable, but the birds took no heed of that, and came there regularly to feed, especially the flocks of starlings.

FREEDOM AGAIN

We shot starlings. We would walk along the fence till we gauged we were opposite the feeding birds, then we banged on the fence to drive them into the air. As they rose, we'd swing the gun up, pick our birds, and shoot for them to fall our side of the fence.

Father was strict as ever with the shooting of us boys.

'Let finger, brain and eye work together,' he would say. 'Put your head down, and look square along the sights. Half the bad shooting comes from not getting the head right down. And kill well in the air.'

He had scraped a hollow in the stock for the cheek to nestle into. He saw that we did what he advised, and under his strict eye we became expert shots, so that Father used to boast about us in his conversation – but only in our absence – we were never good enough for him when we were there.

I was with him shooting on the very morning of my wedding.

We had had early breakfast, for the wedding was to be at nine. And there we were, blazing away, with the church waiting quietly, just across the fields.

Father suddenly looked at his watch: put it back in his pocket. 'Boy,' he said, 'time you were across the road to be married. It's a serious job, getting married. Put that gun in the shed for now.'

We went across to the church together. And later, I went back with him, to the shooting, till dinner time.

After dinner, we were left alone, just my wife and I.

We sat by the fireside, and played records on an old Edison-Bell phonograph with cylindrical records, the only instrument we possessed. We were poor, but rich with the thoughts of our love, and of the years that lay ahead. How hard they were to be no one could guess. But their symbol stood in the corner of the little room, the firelight glinting in it – a new twelve-bore gun, my wife's wedding gift to me, and one for which she had been saving for many months from her earnings.

Wedding breakfast? Wedding cake? We had the wedding cake, a slab of plain shop cake, all we could afford. We could have been no happier with riches. We were secure in each other; we understood one another: I had married the daughter of a net-maker and poacher.

4

I Take Work

WE were married but we had no home of our own. For six months we lived with my father and mother and brothers. Not a penny did I take home and give to my wife; all went into the common pool, for Father was out of a job and none of my brothers was working. Lucky it was for all that I had found a steady job with the Gas Company as fitter, and a good fitter too, so that I could earn four shillings an hour.

When the day at the Gas Works was over I was not idle. At the top of the house Mother had a spare room and there I set up a workshop. People brought me bicycles for repair and cleaning and painting. I bought old machines and odd parts from ragmen's barrows, built them up, painted them and found a ready sale. So I earned a few shillings more and kept the skill in my fingers that loved the feel of a tool. I saw every difficulty as a challenge; and many there were, among the odd pieces of machinery brought to me.

I took up again the watch repairing I had learnt years before in the North. The news went round that I was a man who could do a job well and cheaply, and soon I sat at my repairs to the accompaniment of watches and clocks ticking all around.

I found more customers among the men at the Gas Works. I had laid a bet with them one day that if they would dismantle three watches and stir the parts up in a tumbler, I would have the watches together again and working in under the hour. I won the bet.

I TAKE WORK

Whenever I had a few shillings to spare, I would buy old watches and watch parts and cases, and made good timekeepers to sell. But I was tricked, trying to make bright cases out of old. One Sunday morning in Club Row I saw a man 're-silvering' old articles, among them watch cases. For sixpence I bought a bottle of his mixture and went home to try it out. Very good the effect was, while it lasted, but that was not much more than twenty-four hours. I thought I would try my hand at making a mixture for myself. At work I filched the quicksilver from some of the barometers, brought it home and made it up with acid. I shook it well, corked the bottle tight and put it on the table beside me as I worked. I was busy mending a watch when there was a bang. The bottle blew to bits and some of the mixture rose into the air and dropped back down my neck. Never had I moved so quickly to the tap, for cold water to wash the burning acid off.

Now, with work by day and more work by night, there was all too little time to turn away from town to the fields. Yet the chance did come, and I took it. Sometimes with Father or one of my brothers, but mostly alone. Close at hand was the vast expanse of the Sewage Farm, and for the longer hours of freedom Cuffley or Cheshunt, or anywhere within cycling reach where I thought there would be a chance of a bird for the pot.

There I wandered with gun at the ready, or lay in wait, till dusk had crept down on the fields and I knew there was work to be done at home.

Even shooting so close to home as the Sewage Farm brought the excitement the poacher always knows, that of eluding the law, for no poacher keeps within it.

One Sunday morning I had gone there with my brother to shoot, knowing full well that no Sunday shooting was allowed. A couple of snipe went up in front of me. Bang! Bang! One bird fell almost at our feet, the other veered in a wide arc and went down on the other side of the railway line. 'Quick, George,' I said, 'you nip over and get it.'

He was no sooner out of sight than a policeman appeared, having heard two shots.

'Name?' he said. 'Your gun licence?'

'I'm shooting on Father's licence.'

'Name and address, please.'

'Smith, 6 Wray's Avenue.' I knew no Smith was there, the place was empty.

Just then, over came George with the dead snipe. He sized up the situation as the policeman turned to him. There was no need even to give him a wink.

'Your name Smith?'

'Yes, sir.' Like a shot.

'And you live at No. 6 Wray's Avenue?'

'Yes, sir.'

We felt the policeman had asked for that. The rest we left him to find out for himself.

But we were not finished with him.

There came a Saturday. I was shooting with a friend in Pickett's Lock Lane. We were within fifty feet of the highway, the Kingway's Highway as it then was, so were guilty of a misdemeanour in the eyes of the Law.

Sure enough we were caught, and this time it meant Tottenham Police Station; and there, waiting to be called in, I was recognised by the very policeman who had been so interested in the shooting of snipe on a Sunday.

He appeared in court too.

'Your honour,' he began to explain, 'this man eluded me on a Sunday morning some weeks back, on . . .'

The magistrate glanced down at his papers.

'Is this the charge?' he asked.

'No, your honour. . . .'

'Then get down, you are wasting my valuable time.'

He read the charge aloud: 'Shooting, within fifty feet of the King's Highway.'

He glanced at me. I knew a friend when I saw one. 'Guilty, your honour,' I answered smartly, 'and I'm very sorry, it shan't happen again.'

'Five shillings,' he said, 'or five days.'

I paid, and walked out a free man. The policeman was in the corridor. 'All right, Curtis,' he said, 'I'll have you yet.'

I waited for my friend. He came out furious. 'A pound,' he cried. 'A pound or a month.' He had been so sure of getting off, he had argued the case.

I TAKE WORK

I told him my fine was five shillings. He wanted to go back into the court.

'Come on,' I said, 'learn your lesson, you've talked too much already.'

We Find a Home

So the days and nights slipped by till at last we were able to get a home of our own, just two rooms, one upstairs to live in and one on the ground floor that became my workshop.

Small? I felt like a king. I gave up my fitter's job at the Gas Works, and determined to be a watch repairer in earnest, with hours of my own keeping. The Works said I might have the maintenance of their clocks in my care for as long as I wished. Now to me came the watches and clocks, some valuable, some so only to their owners, but all work, which was what I wanted.

An old lady came to me once, bringing a breast-watch for cleaning and repair.

When the job was completed, I was surprised to see her coming in again next evening. 'Nothing wrong?' I asked. No, she just wanted me to wind it for her. And every evening after, for some months, that old lady made the journey to my shop, arriving at six o'clock to have her watch wound. I made no charge for so small a service, but how much it meant to her she showed in other ways, for every now and again there would come for me a pair of hand-knitted socks, or a knitted tie.

Another time there came a big old navvy, with a railway timekeeper. Could I clean it for him? Yes, I said, and the charge would be one and sixpence. I knew the type of watch – cheap. Sure enough, when I came to examine it, I found on every spot on the metal plate where a spindle came through, a blob of red paint to simulate a jewel.

I dropped the plates into my cleansing mixture of benzine and whisky. When I came to brush them with my watchmaker's brush every trace of red paint vanished, to leave the plates bright and clean.

The navvy came for his watch. 'Is it done?'

'Yes, it's ready,' and I handed it to him.

He opened it, looked up with a face like thunder on a sunny day. 'Where's my jewels?'

'What do you mean, jewels in a two-and-sixpenny timekeeper?'

He didn't stop to answer, but landed me a blow between the eyes. He looked like a madman about to wreck the shop.

'Hold on a minute!' I yelled, and dived my hand into a drawer where I had one or two similar watches. 'Is this like yours?' I held one out for his inspection.

'Of course it is.'

'Then look.'

I dipped a matchstick into my solution, rubbed it on the red spot and removed it. I cleaned away another, and another.

'That satisfies me,' the navvy said, 'now I've somebody else to see. When I came in to you I'd just paid twenty-five shillings for that watch, in a pub.' I was glad I was not the man he was going to see.

Another time, as the gas man was in the kitchen carrying out a repair the door opened and two youths stood there, without entering. 'Interested in a gold ring, guv'nor?'

'Where is the ring?'

They handed it to me. It was gold right enough, set with five diamonds.

'What do you want for it?'

At that instant the gas man called out some question from the kitchen – a great gruff voice breaking in – and I was alone, the youths had bolted. I ran to the doorway in time to see them going for all they were worth down the street.

'Very strange,' I thought, 'but they'll be back.'

But they didn't come, that night or any other night.

At last I put the ring in a tray in the window, and there it remained, unsold. When it became obvious that no one was going to claim or to buy it, I took the diamonds out, and sold them on the kerb in Hatton Garden for five pounds each. The ring I melted down with other oddments of gold, placing it in a piece of hollowed coke, and heating it with a blowlamp.

Gold, in those days, was not hard to come by. I recall the dismantling of the White City. Men coming off work would

I TAKE WORK

carry lumps of cornice away with them. They took it round to the messroom, and there scraped off the covering of gold leaf. The leaf was taken to a jeweller, who melted it and ran it off into little solid blocks. These the jeweller would weigh and buy, and the men shared the proceeds.

Little by little my business grew. My only grumble was that people were so slack in collecting their timepieces.

The days ran on towards Christmas, and still I had a shopful of unclaimed pieces. Christmas Eve came. 'Sally,' I said to my wife as I opened the shop, 'if they come today we'll have a real Christmas for the children.'

But they did not come. All day I sat, finding little tasks to take my mind off things, looking up at each oncoming step only to hear it go by.

Morning, afternoon, tea-time.

Sally called me up for a meal. It was little real appetite I had, wondering where the Christmas dinner was to come from. 'Sally,' I said, 'if nobody turns up within the hour, you'd better try to borrow from your father. What a Christmas for the children!' For by now we had a family: we should never be able to face them in the morning with nothing for Christmas Day.

Then, before I had finished eating, there was commotion down below and a knocking on the counter. I hurried down. The shop seemed full of people all come for the same thing, the clocks and watches they had left forgotten for so long: and they kept coming. Eighteen pounds I cleared, and not a watch was left in the shop.

'Come on, Sally,' I cried eagerly up the stairs, 'we've just time for the presents.'

I started putting things to rights in the shop when the door opened once more and a soldier walked in.

'Have you a watch for sale, a good one?' he asked.

'Sorry, I haven't a watch in the shop.'

'I wanted one badly,' the soldier went on, looking round helplessly. 'What about this?'

He pointed to a watch I had on the counter, not for sale but used for checking other watches by. It was one I'd been given, out of order, just as it had come from the effects of an old man who had died. It was a good English lever, and I had set it to rights, and valued it. 'You can have it for two pounds,' I said.

He picked it up, glanced at it with a curious expression on his face, then opened the back and read the inscription there.

In silence, he pulled out a roll of pound notes, took off three and placed them on the counter. He looked at me. 'You can keep the extra for a drink,' he said. 'I've been away in India and now the first watch I buy on my return belonged to my dead father. You could have had any price you liked to ask.'

I was sorry to part with the watch, but not for the manner of its going. Somebody else had found his Christmas too.

Now, with the short days and the dark evenings time was all too brief for out-of-doors. Yet I took my toll in those hours. I filled my lungs with wintry air, I drew great breaths into lungs too long bent over the watchmaker's bench; hours when the skill of my fingers lay strong yet trigger-light upon the gun. Duck, snipe, starlings, larks, blackbirds, thrushes, anything that flew and that was edible, I shot.

Back to the Fields

Times were to change once more.

The woman in whose house we lived suffered from ill-health. Two husbands she had already had, and both dead from tuberculosis. Now she married a third, a great strong man, a docker, and he followed the others.

Then her eldest daughter, grown up to be eighteen or nineteen, a beautiful young woman, died too. The mother could bear no more of that place, but went away to London, and left us sole tenants.

Before long the landlord, finding us there, gave notice to quit. I tried all I could to persuade him to let us have the whole house. My business had worked up into a nice little living; we could well do with a house. But it was no use. The landlord had other tenants in view. He took me to court, and there I told my tale. The only satisfaction I got was that we were to come to some mutual understanding. We did. I had six weeks to get out.

I TAKE WORK

Now indeed times were grievously changed. For two years I was to live in a slum; a haunt of gipsies and of didicais and flower sellers. A place where donkeys had been kept in the parlour, and where I had seen their heads poking out of the windows. A place where every Saturday night, when they threw men out of the public houses, there was a fight in the road, a fight to which the police never came till it was over. The house was in keeping. Sitting indoors, we could see passers-by, even with the blinds drawn, through the gaps in the wall of the front room. Gone was my watchmaker's business, gone any hope of ever starting it here. How could I ask a man wearing a gold watch and chain to risk coming to such a place?

Now, to make a living, I turned to the life I had always longed for: to bird-catching in the fields, to snaring for the cage-bird market, and to shooting for the pot. My days I lived out of doors. When times demanded I lived nights there too. When I tell you that not once in all the two long years I was in that slum did I visit the primitive sanitary arrangements, you will understand.

As day broke, I would come in, to the one room that served as bed and living room. I was cold, I was empty, but usually there was something I had brought for the day ahead. I would squeeze past the big bed that slept us all, and softly put the gun in the corner. Sally would motion me to table. I squeezed in again between bed and table, on to the wooden bench that served us for chairs. And there, unwashed, unshaven, with sleep tugging me down, I sat to eat, in a dream of places and sights far away, yet home, and glad to be there; and Sally's love was like a warmth in the room.

Little by little, as the circumstance of finance allowed, I got together my apparatus; the tackle I should need as a professional bird-catcher, and, most important, nets of every description. Sally's father was an old poacher and a first-class net-maker; we would sit together of an evening making my nets. Anything he made for me I paid him for. But what he taught me out of a life-time of experience, I could not have bought anywhere at any price. All the wrinkles of the net-maker's art he showed me, and to them he added hints on the setting and the use of nets. He made me the finest and lightest pair I ever had – all in silk. The heaviest part of a net is the lines, for drawing it over the birds. Our line was always of sisal, never a sash line or a plaited one that would stretch in use. We burned the rough fibre off the sisal, greased it well, then took it outside and pulled out what stretch there was, if any, around posts. Once so stretched and prepared, that line would never give us an anxious moment. When, down on one knee for efficient working, I pulled, the nets flew over and fell true, every time.

I made a start in a field close to home, in the countryside that has vanished. We were allowed to take, outside the Metropolitan area, many kinds of birds. Some, of course, bird-catchers never took – titmice, and the migrants that require insect food; but any bird that could sing, and live on hard seed, and in a cage, we sought to catch. A walk by any bird shop would show you two or three hundred of them hanging in cages outside. Blackbirds, thrushes, siskins, larks, greenfinches, redpolls, with chaffinches, linnets and goldfinches. The goldfinch, like the plover, was a forbidden bird; but on the other hand it was the bird-catcher's prize – his money-maker – for a goldfinch would always sell: and nobody could prove these to be wild birds.

As my skill increased, and the number of birds left to catch diminished, I began to look around at the country farther afield. I would leave my tackle behind, and find out what the land supported, and where the birds came down to feed, and – most important – on whose land they were.

There were still waste lands then, where I needed to ask no man's permission to lay my nets, but most often I worked on farmland.

When I had made up my mind to see a farmer, I would take off my neckerchief, and put on collar and tie. I would walk up to the house, and the dogs ran out barking to meet me; but dogs I love, and they know who likes them, so that the farmer, looking from his window or the shadow of the barn, saw them cavorting around me eager for favours. Then he would come out and ask my business. I would bid him 'Good day, sir.' Always 'sir' to a farmer, for experience had taught me how far it often took me.

Then I'd ask if he'd mind my catching a few birds on his land. 'To keep them off the crops,' I would add.

'The crops, eh?' What harm should I be doing, was what most of them wanted to know. Here was my chance to tell the tale – and I told it well – how I should do no harm at all, but save the young plants instead.

Sometimes I got a firm but polite, 'No'; at others I would be given permission to catch. One friend I made like this, and friends we remained for years, so that I could always go on to his land, and often did. This friend was Mr. McMullen, a farmer at Cuffley. His was a large farm, with rolling chalkland fields that held for me the sense of spaciousness I loved, and the birds I needed to make my living as a bird-catcher. His was the greatest kindness I received. On occasion I was able to repay him a little.

I was catching chaffinches off a field that had been ploughed and sown with wheat. In the field was a haystack, and there behind it I had laid my nets, ready for the birds as they came in from the field to the stack. As I knelt with line in hand and waited for the moment when I must pull, I kept my eyes as all bird-catchers do, on the birds trafficking back and forth. There were rooks, an unsteady stream of them, coming to an oak that stood in the middle of the field, and from there going down to the ground. I reckoned two to three hundred were in the field.

Then, as I watched and waited, I became aware of a voice talking somewhere behind me. 'Oh dear, oh dear,' I heard, 'the blasted things will ruin me!'

I went to the corner of the stack and looked round; it was Mr. McMullen.

'What do you mean?' I asked. 'Who'll ruin you?'

'Why, just look at that field. That's my wheat – I shan't have a blade left growing by the time those birds have finished.'

'Those birds' were the rooks, going from plant to plant, pulling up the four inches of green, eating the root, and throwing the rest away.

'Look at them, digging them up. Can't you do anything about it, keep them off, or something?'

'Have you got a gun in the house?'

'Yes, but the only man who can use it is my son, and he's away from home, laid up sick.'

'Will you trust me to use it?'

'Yes. There's plenty of cartridges. I'll go and fetch it.'

'No,' I said, 'not today. Leave the gun in the barn for me if you will, and I'll collect it tomorrow morning before it's light. I'll tell you what I could do with, and that's a few sacks and a ladder.'

'I'll get them now,' he said, and went off to do so.

When he came back, I said I'd have a walk out to the field, and off I went, with ladder and sacks. The oak I had seen was a thick, sturdy tree. I climbed into the crown, and had a look out; it was just what I wanted. I broke off a branch or two to allow of a clear view of some twenty yards out into the field, then I arranged the sacks to make a comfortable kneeling place, for I shoot best on one knee. There would be little scope for moving once I was in place next morning.

I had done all I could there in the field. I went back to the haystack and made ready for home. The nets and birds I carried into the barn. When I was catching there was no need to take home all my birds, only the freshly caught ones. My call-birds and brace-birds, used to lure the wild birds down, I left in the barn with food and water for twenty-four hours.

'Sally,' I called as soon as I got in, 'have we any cardboard in the house?' We hadn't a piece. So after tea I set off and begged cardboard boxes from the shops. I took them home and set to work, and after a few attempts I could cut out a rook life-size, with a wedge keel at the base to push into the ground. Then, with a mixture of Cherry Blossom boot polish and soot we gave the rooks a fine black shine. Twelve nice dummies I made, and very handy they were to be in the years ahead.

I rose in the chill hours, and by daybreak was in my oak tree. There beside me on the sacking lay the gun, and the cartridges in a hat. And there in the field outside were the dummy rooks facing in all directions. I settled myself in comfortably, ready for the wait, and congratulating myself on the rooks, which looked real from thirty or forty yards away, only they didn't move.

Then, as the sky began to get light, I heard, 'Waah. . . .

Quaah', from the rookery not far away. The birds started to come. They saw the dummies. They flew over, and the dummies 'vanished'. I could see the rooks turning their heads from side to side in puzzlement. They turned back; fifteen, fourteen yards away: and now the slaughter started. I shot; I killed two, perhaps three, and away the rest would go, but others would be down again within ten minutes, though farther out in the field; I had only to wait. They were so used to feeding there, they seemed unable to leave; and still those dummies stood there unperturbed. By breakfast time I had killed twenty-seven, and the rooks had gone. I came down and made over to the gate where Mr. McMullen had just arrived. I was carrying a bundle of dead rooks, some already lousy with vermin leaving the cooling feathers. He stared at my bundle; the biggest bunch of rooks he'd ever seen dead in his life, he said. He looked out over the field towards the tree. 'Look, Alf,' he cried excitedly, 'they're out again.' They were the dummies. I took him to see them. 'Ah,' he said, scratching his head, 'you're a cunning one, Curtis.'

'Right,' I said. 'Now if we can get five big sticks, I'll show you something else.'

He brought them. They were about six feet long. I put one in each corner of the field, and one in the middle, and to each stick I tied one of the old birds with grey face, head down, and hanging loose on some six inches of string. People will tell you that it makes no difference, that rooks ignore their dead hanging there, but I tell you that it worked – that Farmer McMullen had the finest crop of wheat from that field that he had harvested for many a year.

About two years after, I remember, a farmhand – a man who always took his harmonica into the fields with him to play, was ploughing that very field, when the earth collapsed at one spot, and a cavity appeared, a seemingly bottomless pit. Every kind of rubbish and waste was thrown into it without effect. One day I crawled out over it on a plank held by three men, to see what I could of the bottom; nothing! It was evidently a chalk working, a relic of the old days, like the tunnels into the chalk which we knew of, but into which we dared not venture for fear of their collapsing.

It would be about this time, when I was helping with the threshing, that I said to Mr. McMullen, 'Do you mind if I have the waste seeds – the wild seeds – for my birds to feed upon?' He gave me permission at once. 'Take all you want,' he said. 'Bag up the lot, you can have them always.'

This was a stroke of good fortune. I had all the seeds the birds needed: knobweed – you probably call it knapweed – thistle, plantains, clover, chickweed and groundsel. More than that, I had seed to spare. I put it up into little bags, a tablespoonful per packet, and I took it with me to Club Row where I sold birds until the Society officials drove me out. With each bird I sold, I sold a bag of my mixed seeds, as a bird-refresher or tonic – and a real tonic it was, not like some of the stuff sold today, mere empty husk with no seed left for the bird. Twopence a packet I sold it, and it proved a popular and a regular source of income. So farmer and birdcatcher helped each other.

There came a time when I was able to repay a little more of the farmer's kindness. I was taking birds in this same field, and as usual looking around at the birds of the air. I saw a party of jays slip along the length of a hedge, one behind the other in the manner of jays, just a white glimpse of rump and a rise up into a tree. The whole length of the hedge they went, and vanished into the spinney at its end. I waited, and sure enough, one after the other, still in silence, out they came and down into the field to eat the seed. They were there again next morning, but I was in the spinney watching for them with a gun, and oh what a surprise awaited those jays!

Sometimes, if things went well, or if I thought they would change, I would be bird catching all day; at others, I would gather up my tackle after midday and take the gun to get dinner.

Mr. McMullen gave me permission to take the rabbits on his land; I needed no second invitation. In three weeks I had taken sixty-eight rabbits, by ferreting, snaring and shooting. The gin trap I never used, nor is it ever needed. As soon as rabbits became gun-shy in one spot, I would roam the fields, looking for gaps in the undergrowth, the tunnels where they had left and re-entered, and noting the little pits they dig for

I TAKE WORK

latrines, and the freshness of their droppings on ant and mole heaps.

So I found where to go; but there was one place where with all my trying I could not make a kill. I came to know it as The Firs, for on a steep slope grew two stands of fir trees some ten yards apart, with a heading of rabbit holes under each. I would put the ferret in on one side, but so quick were the rabbits to run, and so short the distance they had to go, they were to safety before I could shoot. If I did risk a shot, I would catch their hindquarters, and over and over the stricken animal would roll, and so down a hole, there to die before I could get to it. Father came one day to give his advice. 'Give the rabbits a chance, boy,' he said, 'give them a chance.' The rabbits gave him no chance, and in the end he went home empty-handed. But I wasn't to be beaten by a rabbit. I brought some cardboard with me. I blocked up the holes in one heading with cardboard and a clod of earth on top, then slipped the ferret into a hole on the other side. Out bolted the rabbits. Across they went as usual, and there stopped. They scratched at the hole; and before they could turn about, they died, for I had brought a light gun with me, very quick in execution.

One day Mr. McMullen came to me in a difficulty. He was about to start with sheep. The sheep were on another farm some three or four miles away, his son was still away ill, and there was no one he could send. Would I go? I didn't like to say no. I volunteered, knowing nothing of driving sheep. He gave me a note for the farmer and off I went.

Sure enough, the sheep were ready. 'There they are, boy,' says the farmer, 'all penned ready. Let 'em out! Away you go, they're all there.'

I let them out. What a time I had then. I got behind them, I tried to move them off. They went every way but mine. The farmer was watching. 'Ever driven sheep before?'

'No, sir, I'm a Londoner. I do a bit of bird catching on Mr. McMullen's land, and I'm trying to help him out.'

'Now you do what I say.' He whistled to his dog.

'You just walk in front, and leave the rest to the dog. Walk straight to McMullen's. Look back,' he said, as I pushed through to the front, 'and you'll see they're all behind you.' They were, and the dog at the back of them all. I set off in front. For a bit I worried: then confidence grew in me, and I knew the dog had more knowledge of sheep driving than I should ever have.

We came safely to McMullen's – and a good square meal.

These were days of freedom. In the crispness of the morning I would be already out in the fields, with the fare home safe in my pocket, a sandwich or two and a bottle of cold tea. I could forget hunger for many hours, intent upon my work. There too, with my nets laid out in the beauty of the fields and the need to pit my wits against those of the birds, I could forget the slum I had left behind.

One morning I was in a new spot. My nets were laid ready, twenty yards out, perhaps, alongside a hedgerow. I settled down to wait and to watch, the air for birds, the fields around for their wild life.

Then I heard a new note, full of excitement – the huntsman's horn. I crouched unmoving; it is not being in the open that makes one conspicuous, but movement. And there down the field came Master Reynard himself. He kept along under the hedge till he came to a thick growth of holly, where he leaped up, and ran along its top to an old oak. Into that oak I saw him vanish.

I waited. The noise of the hunt drew near. Through the gate at the top of the field came a huntsman. I drew in the nets in haste. The last thing I wished was to have hounds rampaging over them. The man drew near.

'What are you doing in here?'

'Catching birds, sir.'

'Have you any right?'

'Certainly I have, I shouldn't be catching them otherwise.'

'You haven't seen anything of the fox, I suppose?'

For a moment I was half inclined to say, no, I hadn't.

'It's funny, we always seem to lose him here,' the man went on.

'Well, I know where he is.'

'You do what?'

'He's in that oak.' I pointed it out.

'Well,' exclaimed the man, 'I'll be . . .'

The field went into action. The hounds were called back from their circling – some as far out as the lane, where they had gone in the effort to pick up the scent they had lost at the holly hedge. A man climbed the tree and peered into the hollow, and there was Master Reynard. A spade was brought, and a hole enlarged at the base of the tree. It was not long before Reynard was out, and caught and killed, and his brush cut off. I had no pleasure in that part, for although the fox is an enemy to the farmer, and although I have taken more than my share of the wild life of the land, yet I have killed to eat, or to earn a living, not for sport.

I was given five shillings for my tip. 'Do you know anything about gates?' I was asked. No, I said, but I could open and shut them, and I agreed to do so, whenever the hunt came.

Now, when I knew there was to be a meet in the district, I left my bird-tackle in the barn or at home, for I could go home thirty shillings the richer in a day, simply opening and shutting the right gates: with a shilling from the first man through, and a half-crown from the last.

And still most days in the season, I was bird catching.

I remember one hot day. I was catching nothing. The hours went by, the sun climbed, the heat fell without a breath. Thirst grew unbearable, I had no drink with me, I was some way from the farmhouse, and I did not like to leave my nets untended. I searched around for water and found some in a moat-like depression. It was covered with duckweed. I stooped and brushed some away with my hands, and the water below lay clear and pure. I drank and was refreshed. I went back to my bird catching. That afternoon I remember, but none of its details. What with the heat, and my emptiness, and the water that must have been bad after all, I was violently ill. It seemed hours before I could find the strength to get my tackle together and stagger up to the house. Mr. McMullen listened to my tale. 'Take a good long drink of milk,' he said. I picked up a can and had a good drink: I felt better – it was cream I'd been drinking. There was no more catching for that day. I had missed my train home, I could not get another till mid-evening. I thought I would try for a rabbit for supper. I knew where there would be some – sitting out on the far side of a hedge in the quiet of the evening, but unfortunately on forbidden land. I walked softly down the lane, and looked over the hedge. From the grass a pair of ears lifted, and my gun lifted in the same instant; the rabbit was mine. I gave a glance round, and crept through the hedge to pick it up. Just as I laid hold of it, my eye caught a movement in a tree ahead; something had leapt up into it. I went over and peered up, to see two green eyes staring down. In a flash the gun was up, and I emptied the second barrel. Down together fell a rabbit and a large cat, both dead. A very large cat, striped like a tiger, with bob tail and crop ears. I bent down to pick it up and look more closely. 'What are you doing here?' A Keeper. As if he didn't know, having heard the shots.

I showed him what I'd shot: the rabbit and the cat.

Now there came another shout from the hedge. 'What's the matter, there?' The Keeper's employer came over. He gave a glance. 'You've got him then. That's the explanation. A lot of people have been blamed for the going of the pheasants. Get up into the tree, George, and have a look.'

George got up. He gave an excited shout. 'Must be a hundredweight of bones and feather and fur up here! Rabbit and pheasant.'

He came down, and in silence the two rabbits were picked up, and the cat. 'Come up to the house,' I was told. This, I thought, is the bad end to a bad day. But I told my tale, of how I had been bird catching and fallen ill, and how I had tried to take home at least something to eat. Then the gentleman had wine and biscuits brought to me; and when I told him I was allowed to keep down the rabbits on Mr. McMullen's farm opposite, he promised I should shoot the two or three hundred yards of hedge along the road edge and that led from the spinney where the rabbits bred. Tuesdays and Fridays I might shoot, and take no pheasant or game: though I was allowed ferrets. I came home, happier at heart than I had been at any time that sorrowful day and with two rabbits, and a certain source of meals to come.

Another day I was at McMullen's all ready to go bird

I TAKE WORK

catching, when a newcomer approached. 'Are you the bird-catcher?' he asked. I said I was. 'Very pleased to meet you. I'd like to come along and see how you do it.' It was the farmer's son who had been away ill so long.

'Right,' I said, 'you come along with me tomorrow. I'll be taking chaffinches again then. I'll be there from daybreak on.' I was there at the first greying of the night, but the young farmer, with no need to rise with the sun, did not turn up till ten in the morning.

I had laid my nets where I knew I could take some birds. In the nets, between them as they lay ready to sweep over, was a brace-bird, used to draw others into the net space. The brace itself is a tiny light harness made from chamois leather and fitted with a tiny swivel at its base, so that the bird can turn at will. It has complete freedom of movement except that it is linked to the flirt stick, on which it perches and from which it flutters down to drink or to feed – for always within reach of the flirt stick and below it are little conical containers of seed and water pushed into the ground.

Many stupid, and wrong, criticisms have been made of the putting of a brace on to a bird, but I say this, and I will prove it to you, that properly put on by a man who knows what he is about, the brace allows perfect freedom of movement and of flight. Not the professional, but the fumbling amateur and those who knew nothing of it, made cruelty of the brace. The professional depended on his birds, they were his whole livelihood. Do you think he could draw other birds down to be caught, by showing a bird in distress? I would take home a wild bird, put it in my aviary, and then in late evening take it out for training to the flirt stick. Four hours it would take me, with hands that were always gentle, and with infinite patience. At the end of those four hours the bird had no fear of me or the flirt stick, on which it sat as if on a wild twig.

All this I was explaining to Alastair, the farmer's son, for now that he was come he was interested in all he saw, and soon had noticed the bird on its perch in the net. I was catching well: every five minutes or so over would come the nets, eighteen yards long by five feet high, and catch a few more.

Alastair stood behind me, looking about eagerly. 'Look

out,' he cried, 'here comes another lot – make your bird jump about a bit.'

This was just what I did not do. All I did was pull the string that ran from the flirt stick to raise the stick gently into the air, and wait for the birds to come right over. Then gradually I lowered the flirt, my bird opened its wings and fluttered gently to ground. Now the birds overhead, seeing as they thought a bird settling between the nets, followed it down: and over them fell my clap nets. Five out of six I had caught. The sixth, not quite low enough to be caught, twisted around the edge of the net, and was out and away. With that one escape he had learnt a lot: he had become what was known to professionals as a sharp bird, one educated to the nets, and very hard ever to take again. A bad bird for us to have free in a flock.

And now I have told you of the art of taking birds with a brace-bird and a flirt stick – an art that from beginning to end calls for patience, gentleness and skill. No man worthy of the name of bird-catcher was ever anything but gentle with his birds.

One more bird-catching story.

I used to go to The Plough at Cuffley for a drink and a bite of bread and cheese when times would allow of it. At the back of the pub was a small paddock with a pony; a field full of knobweed. And over that knobweed went a drove of some twenty goldfinches – birds that had earned quite a reputation. They were the talk of Club Row, where men swore that if only they had the time to come down, they would surely catch them. All the same two or three London professionals had tried, without success. I said to the publican, 'Can I have a go at those goldies?'

'You can have a go. You'll do no better than the other boys.'

I tried. Those goldies were so sharp I declare they could have set up nets for themselves. They were like the birds left at the end of the catching season; the sharp birds left by March, as time for nesting comes on. I drew a blank. I just couldn't get near them. I had good nets, the best. I had a splendid brace-bird, a hen as all brace-birds were; and in

I TAKE WORK

cages around, I had cocks, singing birds to draw the others down. I went again, and took a friend: and again we failed. No matter where in the paddock I placed my nets, the birds saw them and fed elsewhere.

The day slipped away. It was the time for the goldfinches to take their last feed of the day. Soon I should have to give up. I said to my friend, 'Throw some stones, and drive them right out of the field.' He did so.

Hurriedly I re-laid my nets, some twenty yards out from the hedge where I judged they would come back.

'Now,' I said, 'you stand at the far end, in mid-field, and as they come over wave a hankie.'

And there I waited, lines in hand, alert, watching the air just above the hedge.

My call-birds started to sing again from their cages – and I knew they were coming, for a bird hears its own kind long before the human ear picks up a sound.

One bird came alone over the hedge, and over the net. I caught it in the air, for with the nets you can take a bird up to four feet from the ground. I ran over, delighted. 'I've got one,' I cried. And a beautiful bird it was. I took it softly into my hand, and there it was, complete with brace and swivel. 'Ah,' I said to myself, 'I shan't be long now!'

I took my brace-bird from the flirt stick, and put the newcomer there. Two or three little pulls on the string, to move the stick up and down, and she was back to her old job of luring birds.

Back came the others over the hedge, saw their bird, and came in to settle beside her. Eighteen birds I took, a splendid day's work, with ten cocks at five shillings each, and seven hens at half a crown, and a lovely hen as brace-bird, already trained, and worth its weight in gold, and quite unharmed by the brace she had worn so long.

5

The Poaching Life

NOW that Alastair had made my acquaintance he would come often to see me bird catching, and not bird catching only; he would join me at netting and shooting, for the sportsman lurks in most of us, and the poacher too.

In the end I had to find excuses to get rid of him, for good company though he was, and good shot too, whenever he came with me half of what we caught must in fairness go to him; and he had a living already waiting for him, up at the house. My living too I made in the fields, but differently; every rabbit I took, every bird I caught in the net, was pence and shillings to me.

One afternoon I was with brother Bill. I had just started to put the ferret into a hole, when I saw Alastair coming up the lane. There was no use trying to avoid him, he was sure to look over to the hedge and see us crouched on the bank.

I nudged Bill. 'Alastair's coming. Pretend I'm drunk!'

By the time Alastair caught sight of us, I was reeling about the bank as half-drunk. He stared a moment then called out, 'Mind if I join you?'

'Pretend not to hear, Bill, just throw me up a cartridge into the air.'

Bill pulled one out of his pocket and threw it up and up went my gun. Bang! What a shot! Within seconds the sky was raining lead pellets into the leaves all round; a lucky pellet, as I had hoped, had caught the cap of the cartridge. When the hail was over Alastair called, 'You're not safe to be with, Alf!'

He motioned Bill over and asked what was the matter with me. 'Only a drop too much, I think,' says Bill with a knowing look.

'I don't think I'm staying,' says Alastair, and that was the last we saw of him for that afternoon. It was to be a strange time, and one that went to show that however much we may know of rabbits, or of any other wild creature for that matter, there is always more we can learn.

The afternoon started slowly, with scarcely a rabbit bolting. We had almost finished one bury. 'Put the ferret in and give it one more try,' I said. This was our polecat ferret, dark brown with a pale muzzle, like a wild polecat only smaller.

Bill put it to the hole and in it slipped, while I stood back some fifteen to twenty yards, ready. Scarcely was the ferret out of sight, than a rabbit bolted out in hot haste. I fired; in haste too, only to my chagrin to see the rabbit go. It made for a heading of holes some hundred yards away on the edge of the field. It ran slowly while I waited, watching. Then, before it reached the holes, it swerved away, made a wide detour and came back towards me. And there, at a spot where one thistle stem stood, it sank down and skulked. I loaded up and walked towards it, waiting to see it get up and run. There was no move. I stood over it, picked it up; it was already dead. One pellet from my shots had destroyed the sense of balance. It had run back to its killer.

I walked to where Bill was standing near the ferreted holes. He motioned for silence. 'Look at this, Alf, a big old doe's been going to come out of that hole. I've seen her head come out three or four times.' (You can always tell a doe from a buck, the buck has the broader head.)

'If she does it again she's mine!' I whispered.

And even as I spoke of it up came the head once more. Bang! No undue haste this time: 'Go and get her Bill, that's one each.'

Bill picked up the rabbit, then the ferret which appeared just after: and when we looked at the rabbit there was the explanation of the puzzle, for its hindquarters were a terrible mess: the ferret had been holding on to it, and biting it at the rear, and pulling it back every time it tried to escape. The ferret's wild cousins, the stoat and weasel, will do the same if they corner a rabbit in a burrow.

But that was not all the tale. Some of the lead shot had gone down the hole and a pellet had destroyed one of the ferret's eyes: the ferret would be no more use to us that day. Bill, who can neither read nor write, can do anything with animals. He took the stricken creature down to a tiny stream, bathed the wound and took out the shot, and went off home with the ferret – and in two or three weeks it was working as well as ever. Whenever we were after rabbits, that ferret went with us, its only drawback being its colour, so dull that on a dark night it was invisible, but it never left another rabbit in a hole, but always tried to drag it out.

Another day when we were using it, a rabbit came out, and didn't run, it hobbled. It was so astonishing that for a moment I did nothing, then ran over and killed it with a blow. It proved the fattest rabbit I have ever seen. Well it might be, for it had taken no exercise beyond hobbling out to feed: its legs were gone, all four cut off short. Yet that rabbit had lived, going on the four stumps some terrible accident had left it.

And so the days went by, and we took our toll. We were not the only rabbit-killers on McMullen's farm. There were the two dogs, Peggy and Jack, two little Aberdeen terriers. I got to know them well, with the help of bread-and-butter from my sandwich pack. They lived a life almost independent of man, but once they had confidence in me they followed me about the fields, for I lived the life they lived. Above all, they were filled with doggy joy at the sight of the gun under my arm. I would walk around the fuzz, the gorse bushes as you would call them, the two dogs in front of me. Peggy would smell a rabbit, or hear it move in the thickness of the bush. She gave one sharp bark, and crouched, watching. Jack pushed in and worked the thicket, driving the rabbit till it bolted to where Peggy was waiting. I waited too, with the gun, but as often as not the rabbit was in Peggy's jaws and the cartridge saved. I remember once the dogs went to Cuffley with me: I took thirteen cartridges and came home with ten and nine rabbits, six of them caught by the dogs. Sometimes when I've been out at night around the farm, long-netting, I have seen these two faithful friends going towards home, Peggy ahead, carrying the rabbit they had caught between them, for supper.

Then one day I heard that Mr. McMullen was to get rid of the little bitch, Peggy. I asked him how much he wanted for her. 'She's with pups,' he answered.

'Well how much do you want?'

'Four pounds.'

I said I would have her, and I did, and fetched her away home to Edmonton, and made her comfortable and gave her a nice warm box to have her litter in.

But Peggy had no use for comforts, for she had lived the hard way, never coming indoors at the farm to sleep, but finding what shelter she could from the night. Not even to litter had she taken advantage of man's shelter, her first puppies she had brought forth in a fox's den, with only the bare earth to lay them on. So now she scorned the box, went out into the little yard that was all we had for garden, and there in the mud and wet dug her nursery and bore her pups. There are those who believe that a dog at such a time requires comfort, care, and the attention of human beings: but good stock and mother-love are all that is needed. Out of that mud and wet came the finest dog I have ever had, or ever shall have.

But now, what with the long nights and the bitter exposure I had undergone, illness overtook me. I developed pneumonia and was taken to Silver Street Hospital.

While I was away Sally my wife looked after the dogs, and so I heard the first news of the puppies. Sally came in to see me. 'Peggy's had three pups,' she told me, 'and there's one, a dog you must keep for yourself: it's staggering about carrying one of your old socks.'

That, I made up my mind, would be the one. I lay there in the hospital bed and dreamed of training it, and felt it crouching warm beside me in the wet grass as the sun came up over the hedge and tilted the tree shadows down the field.

I remember that hospital always, and my wife Sally will remember it always, with good reason. I had been for some days on the danger list, when word came by a policeman bearing a buff form stating that I had passed away. The bottom dropped out of Sally's world. In the torment of grief she hurried round to the hospital, only to find it was another Curtis, a Roman Catholic, who had died opposite me in the ward. The relief was almost as great a blow as the news, but for years Sally carried that certificate around with her, a talisman against disaster.

In the meantime I had taken a turn for the better, and at last was home again. And there waiting was the little dog that Sally's intuition had picked out for me, a Tomummer, a little thing.

I was weak for some time, but no sooner did I feel the strength coming into my legs than I began on his training. For a while indeed, I had two dogs, for one puppy I had sold was brought back as a most unruly dog. It seems he had smashed a mirror jumping at his own reflection. In a month I sent him back, perfectly trained. The first thing a dog learns is who is master, and once learnt it is never forgotten, but he does not learn by the thrashings they had tried.

I wanted to get the puppies to come to me, not when they wanted, but at my wish. I would buy a breast of mutton for threepence, or fourpence-halfpenny, or even sixpenny-halfpenny. (It was nothing unusual in those days for the butcher to wrap a piece of the target, the breast of mutton, around the week-end joint.) The puppies soon knew where to come for a titbit. Then they had to learn both to fetch and put down the catch when brought. Many a dog that will fetch has a mouth so hard that the bird when brought is not worth the picking up, useless for dinner. 'Bring!' I would command, the signal I was always to use for the dog to fetch, just as it was 'Go!' for it to drive. But my dogs must be ready to do all I wanted without a spoken word, so they must learn to obey an arm signal, and this they learned next. In the same way, they would fall in behind me at the word, 'Back!' or drop the same fifteen paces behind at the sweep back of an arm. And always, when they did well, there was a word of praise and a pat.

I had one word too, when the dog returned with the find; never 'Drop it!', just 'Dead!' and the bird was placed at my feet. If I was ratting, and the rat bolted, then I might go to two words, 'Here goes!' and the dog knew what was afoot.

I trained my dogs to carry without chopping the bird, with the

THE POACHING LIFE

help of a starling. The skin of a starling is bitter to the taste, as we had learnt when as boys we killed and cooked and ate starlings, but always skinned them first. The starling I used for the dogs was all skin, stuffed with pins. I would throw it up into the air, fire off the gun, and command, 'Bring!' My own little dog, my little Tomummer, my Brinnie as we called him because he was brindled of coat, had one of the loveliest mouths I have known in a dog. He would bring a bird and lay it at the word 'Dead!' at my feet, unharmed. Indeed more than once when I have winged and not killed, Brinnie has laid the bird at my feet and I've seen it get up and run, but only till Brinnie caught up with it and brought it to me once more, this time into my hand.

A poacher's dog is not trained to hunt on his own, but when I was away from home, Brinnie occasionally did so. I well recall how once I came in and missed his welcome. 'Brinnie not home?' He was not, and it was some hours before we heard his scratch at the door; and there he was with a duck in his mouth: and back he went time after time until four more had been brought home. Where he caught them I never tried to discover. Yet, for all his tender mouth Brinnie could kill. At the word of command he would hunt out and kill a rabbit. He would have killed a cat too, had he been told, for all his lack of size – gone back and killed at the word of command as a poacher's dog will.

He proved his courage one night when I was coming home from duck shooting. I had to cross a big patch of rushes some quarter-mile square. There were ducks sleeping on pools of water hidden in the rushes, so I walked with gun at the ready towards the moon, so that the birds must get up against the light. (One should always be careful of sending a dog through rushes at night; I have seen them come back from swimming with eyes badly lacerated.)

When I came out of the rushes with the weight of ducks grown heavier, I had to pass a big half-filled-up pipe that lay upon the ground. In the light of the moon I saw something flash into it. 'Go!' I said to Brinnie. He needed no more telling, but was after that shadow. Now from the pipe came the most terrific din: I called to Brinnie to come out, and out he came, covered with scratches and bleeding badly. I brought him home under my coat, and washed the wounds. The next day I returned to the pipe to see what there was that had given Brinnie such a tussle.

I peered into the darkness of the pipe, and dimly made out something at its end, something still. I got my poacher's hook of barbed wire, pushed it along inside, twisted it into the bundle and slowly drew it out: a huge tortoiseshell cat, dead. Now I understood Brinnie's wounds; and glad I was to see the cat dead, not alone for Brinnie's sake, but because a cat taken to the wild is the most terrible of poachers. This one had evidently taken up abode here in the pipe. I could ill afford to have it live, for there would be little enough left for me with such a rival.

Often in the late afternoons I would go off rabbiting, and there would be Brinnie sitting on the cross-bar of the bike where I had fixed a pad for him, forepaws on the handlebars. Many a quiet lane around Cheshunt, Cuffley and Wormley has seen his eager face as we cycled innocently along. At times on a quiet road we would meet the village policeman. He would give me a glance, catch sight of Brinnie sitting there, and smile good-naturedly. He saw nothing but a happy couple there together on the bike. If ever such a thought entered his head, well, surely a little dog like that could never catch a rabbit! In fact, Brinnie could, but that was not the reason for his presence. Brinnie was there to drive the rabbits into the nets I should lay; and from the first rabbit I took from the net he would have the liver as reward for his service.

But there were other times when coming home as day looked over the world with drawn face, I met the same policeman and he showed suspicion. 'Hoi, just a minute!'

Then I pretended not to have heard aright. 'Half-past four! Half-past four!' I would call out, and pedal for all I was worth till far enough away or out of sight.

There are times of course when a poacher must not be seen with his dog – times when the dog must slip off unobserved at a touch or whisper and make his own way home.

That Brinnie would do so I found out by chance.

One morning I set off for Cheshunt by my usual route,

along the towpath by the River Lee, with Brinnie on the bar and now a constant companion. When I reached the lock at Cheshunt, Peggy, the lock-keeper and a good friend, came out to tell me that he had seen two ducks drop into a swamp some two or three hundred yards away. I called to Brinnie, and off we went. I knew the place well; plenty of rushes and little depth of water.

Nothing had gone up by the time I had reached the spot where I thought they would be, so I sent the dog in to drive, and within a few minutes up got the ducks. I timed my shots; left-pause-right; and dropped both birds. Which prompts me to say a word on shooting with two barrels: most misses are due to over-eagerness, to failure to time that second shot; it is fired before a second sight is taken. There is always more to miss than to hit, it is the sky, the whole world, and only two little ducks.

Well, Brinnie fetched me one duck and went back to look for the second. When he did not come, I began to wade through myself trampling noisily, with the water no more than knee-high up my waders. Back and forth I went among the rushes, till stepping back I trod on Brinnie, who had crept up out of nowhere, unheard and unseen. He yelped in pain, and as so often when we have hurt something we love, I lost my temper and shouted to him, 'Get out of it!' Almost at the same moment I heard the duck and ran in the direction of its flapping, for it was what we call a runner, one that has been winged, unable to fly but still swift on its legs. One goes straight after a runner, for if given a chance it will hide and skulk in silence, but kept on the move by the tramping of feet it gives itself away. There it was now, trying to hide away in the base of the rushes. I called to Brinnie, 'Bring!' No answer. No Brinnie. I got the duck myself, and went back with it to Peggy's, thinking the dog might be there. He was not, so I knocked to ask if Peggy had seen him. Yes, he said, Brinnie was gone off along the Lee path towards Waltham; and when I reached home there he was, waiting to greet me with wagging tail. I could not scold him, he had done as he thought I had commanded; all the lonely miles back I had sent him, unwittingly. Now that I knew, whenever I wanted him to go home I sent him off with a proper word of command, not in anger. Many is the time when I've been out all night rabbiting I've sent him off with a little note in his collar, telling Sally when to expect me; and never did he fail.

On Netting Rabbits

I was at McMullen's again when Alastair came over to me. 'Alf,' he said, 'I'm thinking of getting some rabbits with long nets. I wonder whether you'd like to come?' I didn't tell him that I'd been netting rabbits while he was still at College.

'I'm ready to try,' I said. 'Whose nets are you using?'

'We've got a net up in the barn; one Father took from a poacher,' said Alastair slyly: 'and I know just the place to go, Lady Eaton's; it's swarming with rabbits.' The rabbits, he said, came from a spinney and the fields were running alive with them at dusk.

On my next visit Alastair turned up with the net, a sixty-yard affair and a good one by all appearances. Off we went by daylight and had a look around, and hid the net in readiness, and made arrangements for our meeting.

The night came: we met at the farm, Alastair, my brother Syd, and I. It was a night of darkness. The wind that had sprung up with evening had grown from a leaf-whisper to a hard rattle of leaves: a fine night for the taking of rabbits with a long net. For rabbits, with the wind loud in the air, venture farther afield, going two or three fields away instead of a mere forty yards or so from the burrow. The night was all we could wish.

Alastair took the lead and in silence we picked up the net where it had lain unseen. We put it out along the top of the field he chose, some fifteen yards away from the hedge. Syd had brought along an old can and a length of string. Now he tied the can to the middle of the string, with one end of the string for Alastair, the other for himself. Into the can he softly put a handful of pebbles, and the two of them crept into the night down the edge of the field. I waited by the net, knowing in the blind darkness their every move, listening for the first sound that would tell me to be alert and ready for the killing. Now they would be one at each corner of the field,

THE POACHING LIFE

with the string stretched between them, and the can with its pebbles ready to do its work.

Now they were coming, with a fine din made by the can as it was drawn back and forth across the field as they advanced.

And then, striffing through the grass, the rabbits came. I heard the first one hit the net. I ran to it. Nothing there! Another came and another. I swore I could see them. There were more; they hit the net, I heard them strike it; and hither and thither I ran, and never even the tail of a rabbit in my fingers: I was chasing the phantoms of rabbits.

Alastair came running up, with Syd. 'What's the bag?'

'Nothing! They've been here, but I can't catch them!' And with the coming of the grey dawn we saw: the net was punched full of holes where the rabbits had gone through. Our fine net, that had looked so strong, was completely rotten.

'Don't ask me to go there again after what those rabbits have learnt tonight!' I said. But to myself I was thinking differently. I knew just where the rabbits were, it would be a pity to leave them there. I came home with Syd without saying a word, and went straight off to see a poacher, an old acquaintance; a regular poacher, one who did no real work beside; for when he was not actually taking his toll of the fields and woods he was marking down the places where he would later come; gathering briers perhaps for the making of standard roses, and all the time with an eye for the rabbit runs, and the pheasants he would be meeting. He readily agreed to sell me a net, and a good strong one at that. I tested it to make sure this time, and even then he tricked me, for it was only fifty yards in length, not sixty. A poacher could catch his own brother.

A clear ten days I gave those rabbits to forget, then off I set again for Lady Eaton's, with Syd to help me once more, for Syd was always a favourite with me out of doors, quick to size up a situation and never lost his head. I recall once when we were scrumping for apples. Syd had just got through the hedge, when he caught sight of the farmer standing watching.

'Where are you going?' bawls the farmer.

'Back again!' cries Syd, and slips through once more; and so taken was the farmer with the sally, he calls to Syd to come on over and he'll give him some apples.

I could be sure of Syd.

By two o'clock of the morning we were in the spinney, with night turned cold, and once more the voice of wind in trees. But tonight there was no call for anyone to creep downfield with string and can, for I had brought Brinnie with me – as soft of foot as we ourselves, and as silent.

We put up the net again, and my fingers were glad at the sound strength of it.

I whispered to Brinnie: 'Go! Find 'em, boy!'

He vanished in to the vast shadow that was night over the field. We waited. A rabbit came thrumming on the ground. It came, it thudded into the net, and Brinnie followed. We heard it squeal; and now there was no need for Brinnie to drive, for at the sound all the rabbits in the field bolted for home. The net was suddenly jerking alive with leaping forms, and not one rabbit went through.

There was no time for orthodox killing; we ran up and down punching and slaughtering as fast as we could. Forty-five rabbits in less than half an hour: how many poachers, I wonder, can better that? But it was forty-five rabbits to be got away quickly, and in silence. We stripped and hocked them – pushed one hind leg through the other at the joint, and threaded them on our belts. It took us several journeys, working together; till at last rabbits and net were safely hidden in a little spinney on McMullen's ground, and we felt we might take a brief respite. We made a little fire to keep alive the warmth we had acquired, and brewed tea. It seemed scarcely half an hour before we saw the streaks of dawn in the sky, and the sky paling through the trees; we should have to work fast.

And fast we did work, at gutting rabbits. We'd hang one up, slit it from vent to chest with our knives that were sharp as razors, grab it with forelegs and hind, throw it back over the left shoulder, and cast – and out, of their own weight, came all the entrails into the bushes.

A few days later Alastair was walking across his father's land. He came to the spinney and stopped, unable to believe his eyes.

I was there too, bird catching. I saw Alastair come running. 'Quick, Alf,' he cried as he drew near, 'I'll show you something – the poachers have been here again!' He took me to see. 'What a haul!' he said. 'What a haul!' He stared at the bushes in disbelief at all the paunches. 'Like a great tree of pears,' he muttered. Little did he guess, nor did we ever tell him, that these were the very rabbits he himself had lost when they had gone through his net. I could have told him more: of my wrists and hands, swollen and painful with the killing of many rabbits; of how we had got over the puzzle of getting home forty-five rabbit carcases; how we had taken a long morning walk down to a little grocer's near Cuffley railway station and there bought cakes and tea, and after, an egg box. We had returned to the little spinney, carrying the egg box. The rabbits by now were nicely stiffened; we packed them in, carried the box down to the station and had it put in the goods van, and set off for home. There, we sold them for sixpence each – always provided we might have back the pelt; for rabbit skins were sometimes worth more than the meat in those days.

When we were not trapping rabbits in the long net, or taking them in purse nets at the burrows, we shot them; and my little Brinnie fetched them. So often have I shot over his head that his ears were nothing but tatters, for if I sent him in to drive he would stand when the rabbit was out, and so close that some of the shot was bound to touch him. 'Yap!' he would say, then go on and pick up the rabbit.

Brinnie went with me also when I was shooting birds. I have spoken of his lovely mouth, now I must tell of his persistence. He never lost a winged bird. It takes a good dog to find them. I have picked up birds left by so-called sportsmen that were too bad to eat. Partridge and pheasant with shot festered in them or with toes shot away. Bad shooting, and bad dogs; and more cruelty than a good gun ever brings. Brinnie, as I have said, never willingly left any wounded bird or creature. He would climb a bush or scramble as far as he could into a tree to retrieve a fallen bird. Once, after he'd climbed a tree to get a wounded starling, a gentleman who had seen him do it offered me £20 for him, but of course I was not selling.

Another time I was on the Sewage Farm taking the evening ducks. A bird came crashing down, and in the moonlight I saw it disappear into a thicket. I called to Brinnie, 'Bring!' – and off he went. Now the moon went in, but I could follow Brinnie by the sounds of his moving. I waited. There was silence. I waited still, then, when there came no Brinnie and no sound of Brinnie, I called to him, startling myself with the sound of my own voice there in the silence of the night. When there was still no Brinnie, I went to look for him. There was a stream to cross, and many is the time I have jumped it, but in the daylight. Now I pulled up my trousers, and jumped blind, to land in the icy river, with my feet and legs in soft mud. I scrambled out in haste, to find nettles, but after the river I could feel nothing of them on my legs. I pushed on, not bothering to put on boots and socks, for I should have to return. And there, in the middle of the thicket, where a tree grew out of it, I found Brinnie. He was in a fork of the tree, unable to go farther, and there above him wedged in another fork lay the duck just out of reach; but only just, for its breast was plucked bare where Brinnie had stretched up again and again and tried to pull it down.

I got them, dog and duck together, and went back the way I had come, across the river. Now terror lent me wings, the terror of frost-bite. I put back boots and socks, but I might have had no feet for all I could feel of them. I hurried home fast as I could and called to Sally, as I pushed the door, 'Quick, get some mustard and hot water!' Sally was used to emergencies. My feet began to thaw out in the hot water she brought, and then I felt the stings of the nettles start to hurt, and looking down saw my legs were a mass of lumps.

Next morning I looked out upon a silver thaw; the hard frost was over. I went out to see what I could shoot, wearing over my boots thick woollen socks, that I had picked from the shoot on the Sewage Farm, socks meant for the hard wear I was going to give them. There were no plover, but moorhen after moorhen. Brinnie was bringing them, frozen so that they could not move, with wing feathers stuck to the body with ice. I could have spent the day picking up helpless birds. One that Brinnie brought was not moorhen but snipe, frozen to the icy mud by its beak, the ring of ice still on its beak when he brought it to me.

The hard weather returned, and brought a rare chance to us – almost the only chance we could get of taking siskins. They came regularly to spend winter with us, but only really hard weather brought them in any numbers. They haunted the hob trees, the silver birches, that grew inside the grounds of the Powder Mills. One day my friend Jack Hill came to me in great excitement. 'Alf,' he cried, 'I've seen siskins – a mile of them, away over in Rochford Spinney!' Rochford Spinney lay at Cheshunt some four miles from the Powder Mills at Waltham Abbey. We were safe: nobody would stop our catching there. It didn't take long to get ready, for as I say, the siskin was a rare bird to take in the nets. Arrived, we put up our nets one at each end of the spinney.

By ten of the morning I had caught two birds, and those more by luck than skill. Jack came to see how I was getting on. 'I'll give them another three-quarters of an hour,' he said, 'and then if they won't be caught, I'm going home.'

I determined to stay: if a bird is nimble-witted enough to stay out of the net, then the bird-catcher must be cleverer than his birds. I saw what was happening. Down came one bird to feed. Down came a second, but as the second fluttered down, the first was up and off. I decided to catch them singly. I caught five, put brace and swivel on each, and took them home. There, with food and water, I pegged them down to the floor, allowing each sufficient room to move freely without danger of becoming entangled. I left them so for three or four days, going to and fro through their room to train them and get them used to me, for like the redpoll the siskin takes readily to captivity and is one of the easiest birds to train.

On the fifth day I put my five brace-birds into a cage, and went off with Jack Hill to Rochford Spinney once more. There I set up my nets under a big overhanging branch, and pegged my brace-birds within the nets. Siskins are great lovers of blue maw seed. I sprinkled it liberally around inside the net, so that no bird could reasonably miss it. The birds saw. They saw my birds too, my brace-birds, feeding quietly on the seed. They waited for no second invitation. They came, in fives, in sixes, in sevens and eights. Down they came, while I counted – one, two, three, four, five – and over came my nets. I filled my store cage with birds. I was so busy catching that I took no notice of anything else, and then, there was Jack again watching me in amazement. 'I've got 'em, Jack!' I cried in jubilation.

I filled another store cage with birds, and then it was time for home: the bleak wintry dusk was in the trees and the air sharp with frost, but I was rich. Those birds went to London, to Club Row. Eight shillings a pair we got for them. That was one of the plumpest weeks I ever had, with nearly fifty pounds to share between Jack and me. It meant new boots, new clothes: something new for everybody.

Of Rats and Ratting

IT will be hard for you if you live in a town and have a regular job and a regular income, to understand just how we lived, without any regular employment at all. Nothing was too strange or too unpleasant for us to undertake, if it was going to bring food or money or a little pleasure to those at home. I had a family, they had to be fed and clothed; I saw to it that they were. If you feel squeamish over some of the things I tell, you must remember that you too fight for your loved ones in your own way, with your own weapons.

When I was not shooting or fishing or snaring, I would go on to the Sewage Farm at Edmonton. There the dust carts rolled in all day, and there they tipped their rubbish, the waste from the streets and the houses they had visited. Not all waste. There were men who kept themselves alive by the sale of the goods they salvaged from the dust shoot. When the contents were being levelled off (the employment of one man's whole day) amazing things came to light; things thrown away by mistake by people who later wondered what had become of them. I found a sale for much I rescued from oblivion: a fishing rod in its case; a bundle of three hundred rolls of music for a player piano; brass, lead, pictures with the glass broken, dolls' prams, bicycles, bowls, little images, dolls, and toys that I washed and cleaned and hid about the room for the children to find, at home; tin, zinc, alarm clocks that I could put to rights with my knowledge of clock-making, a hundred and one nick-nacks that all turned to money, and so to food for those at home. Don't think I exaggerate over the things I found; there was always something of value. Some districts gave us better value than others. Winchmore Hill carts were more profitable for instance than those from my own Edmonton. You must believe me when I tell you that so many alarm clocks were discarded and found their way to the dump, often with no more than the main spring gone, that I persuaded the man who did the levelling to put aside all the clocks he came across; and when his orange box held enough he would call upon me to tell me where he had hidden it, and go away the richer for his trouble.

And always, as we turned over the wastes of the dump, we found the rats: big fat fellows that flourished mightily on all the foul filth there was. One day, when Bill and I were sorting together, Bill turned over a heap of rubbish, and three rats rolled out, but at second glance we saw that they were puppies, thrown out, drowned. Bill uttered an exclamation, swore he saw one move. He picked it up in his warm hands that are so strong yet can be so gentle, and it moved again; it was alive. Bill took it home, and reared it and trained it – Dinah of the Dust-heap, and the finest ratter for miles around: born, you might say, amongst rats: brought up among them, and could kill fifty to sixty in one evening. I have seen her so tired with killing, that when she put down a rat she had taken into her mouth, it has run off unharmed – her jaws too weary to close upon it. Quick she was in the killing – her training on the dust shoot made her that – for when we disturbed a colony from under the rubbish, they would dive for safety in all directions, while Dinah leaped and bit and dropped, bit and dropped. If we found a nest of baby rats she leaped again and devoured the lot, and we let her, against all theory, for it helped eke out her rations; and not a scrap of difference did it make to her keenness.

Many a dog was trained for ratting in those days, some for business, some for sport. At the week-end men would come with their puppies and young dogs, to the ground at the back of Cook's Ferry Inn public house, and there they would meet with men who could supply rats, and we were there, Bill and I. A man with a puppy would come up and ask if we had a rat

OF RATS AND RATTING

for him. We would ask if the puppy had ever tackled one before. If the answer was 'No,' we knew what to do, and it was Bill's job to do it. He took a rat from the bag and with the hollow end of a door key snapped off two incisors so that the rat could no longer bite; it was ready for the puppy. Sixpence we were paid for a rat like that, and puppy and rat were put down in the open together, and the dog mauled till it killed. The next week without fail the same customer was there, only this time wanting a rat with teeth intact, for which we charged a shilling. The dog might kill swiftly, it might bungle, but it killed in the end, and if the rat bit first, nobody minded at all, for then the dog's spirit flared up and it leaped to the attack, and so became a ratter.

We had another source of income from the rats: the local Council; for they were willing to pay sixpence a tail for them. We provided them with plenty of tails. We would go ratting overnight, chop off the tails on a big stone, tie them up in bundles of twenty-five, and be at the Town Hall next morning for our cash.

Later, by means of a few inquiries, we found what became of our tails after we had left them: they were all sent for burning, handed to the stoker to be destroyed in his furnace. We found him out and had a chat, and the upshot was that he agreed to let us have the tails back for a small consideration. So home went our bundles of twenty-five, and next morning there they were, mixed up cunningly with new tails and ready to be handed in once more. We lived opposite a public house for years, and saw folk go in for their drinks – and we liked one too – yet in all those years we never went for a drink, not even when we saw the very dustmen drinking away the few shillings they had made from their totting. It took all our time and money to bring up our children.

Now I will tell how we came to be opposite the public house and living in a tiny place of our own. We owed it to rats, for had it not been rat-infested we should never have been able to afford even the small rent it would have fetched.

In those days, after the First World War, houses were scarce, as scarce as they are today, and unemployment plentiful, which meant that many people could afford nothing but a cheap cottage and made it harder for me to find one; one not too far away from the fields. Then one day I was standing talking to a poacher, a man who wanted me to go along with him at nights, and I might have gone had I felt it was to be to anybody's benefit but his. To help the argument he said there was a cottage he knew of to let, one that should suit me, for it lay in a lonely part and gave directly on to the Sewage Farm. I made up my mind to have that cottage. 'You'll have to be quick then,' he said, 'there's a woman going tomorrow to have a look at it.' A plan formed in my mind.

That night as dusk shrouded the vast wastes of the Sewage Farm, the rats crept out: I could hear them fighting and squealing over their scavengings. I shot half a dozen of them and put them in a bag. There was no time to lose. Off I went to the little house that suddenly had become my hope and dream; I crept round to the back, and got in through a window. I placed the rat corpses where they must be seen about the living room, then I turned the kitchen tap on full, and flooded the floor. The water would run away through the night, but the room tomorrow would look terribly damp.

I had done all I could. Next morning I was not at the cottage, I was waiting near the office of the landlord. I was waiting for someone, watching out for a woman dressed in black.

I saw her come and go in, and when she came out again with the keys dangling from her hand, I followed. I followed her all the way to the cottage; saw her open the front door and enter. I didn't count the seconds – I didn't have time – before out she came in a hurry, and set off for the landlord's – with the keys. She didn't take long over giving them back, either. I could almost have told what she said.

After I'd seen her leave, I waited some little time, though always keeping a sharp look-out to see that no other prospective tenant should be before me, then in I went to see Mr. Kennet, and ask if he had a little place I could rent.

He looked at me kindly, but doubtfully. Yes, he said, he had a little place, but he had to tell me there were rats.

'Don't you worry over that,' I said, 'I know how to deal with those, I am a rat-catcher.'

OF RATS AND RATTING

'Then,' he answered, 'the cottage is yours for eight shillings a week.' I took the keys.

I found he was right – there were rats, live ones. I shot twenty-seven in the first week after we had moved in our few belongings. I sat in a ditch, the sewerage ditch, at the back of the house, and watched the rats emerge from a hole between our house and the next, and as they came out, I shot them.

There were four cottages in a row there, and what with the noise of the gun and the strange hours I kept, people soon got to know of me. And when they heard that I was a rat-catcher, they would ask me to put the ferret down in their cottage, and let it do as it wished – either kill outright, or drive the rats into the ditch again – for it was thence they came. The ferret might turn up again in any one of the gardens, and then someone would come round to tell me, and I would go and pick it up and put it back into its hutch, ready for the next time.

The cottages were never really freed from rats. As we sat indoors, at twilight, a noise would begin under the boards of the floor. Visitors would look about in apprehension, for now from beneath their feet came the rattle of old tin cans. 'Never mind the rats,' we'd say, 'they're only having their daily game of football.' We had got used to it ourselves, even looked for it. On top of the floor were more tin cans – all flattened out with a hammer and nailed down over the holes the rats had made and were still making, for as I said, we were never free of them. As soon as the weather turned wet, and the ditches on the Sewage Farm began to fill, the rats came into the cottages, for the warmth and comparative dryness. Then indeed there were rats under the boards – until we had retired for the night. Then, if the children had dropped a spot of jam, or left a smear of butter on the cloth, the next morning you could see where the rats had been, for every spot had been gnawed into a hole.

I did get the cottage empty of rats on one occasion, but it was too drastic to do again. I put a length of hose from the dust shoot on to the kitchen tap, and putting the other end into a rat hole, turned on the tap, and flooded under the floor, not stopping until the water seeped up into other holes. For one night we were free, for it took twelve hours for that water to drain away into the ditch, and even then the room was damp. Yet, with all its difficulties and its drawbacks we were happy in that house, and brought up seven children there.

And so, through rats we found our home; and entry into another home. We were talking one day to a man who had asked about ratting, and he went on to tell us that his employer, for he was engaged on repairs at the moment, had asked him to buy four rat-traps, break-backs, for the rats he believed he had in the house. It didn't take me long to persuade him that he was wasting his time, with Bill and myself ready to clear out all the rats anyone might have. He said he would mention us to his master, and we agreed to meet again.

A day or two later he told us that all was settled. His employer wished me to call round and make arrangements for taking the rats. Only one thing he stipulated, no word was to be passed to the Local Authority: he did not want them to know he had rats there. As you will understand he was safe enough on that score. 'I shall be there,' I said, 'with my brother Bill, for we work together at rat catching. You'd better give me the four break-back traps, they'll be no use to your employer. Tell him they've gone, the rats must have taken them together with the bait.'

Bill and I went round and looked over the house, and told the owner there were rats indeed, and plenty of them, though where they were was a mystery to us at present. However, we could soon get over that difficulty. We would have to take up some of the floor boards, since there were no holes that we could see, but we would go through the house systematically, room by room. He was afraid, he said, that he couldn't pay for all that work, but he would pay according to our catch, so much for every rat we took. What was our charge? Ten shillings, we said, for a large rat, but only seven and sixpence for a small one. He was agreed to that, he said, we might set to work as soon as we were ready, and he hoped all the rats would be small ones.

We lost no time in making a start – by going on to the Sewage Farm and there killing five big rats.

We turned up at the house next morning, and the five rats

were with us, though not in view. When the maid came to let us in, we found she was French, with only a limited knowledge of the English language, but with our signs, and her own native wit, she soon understood what we had come for, and let us into the room we were to work first, the box room.

There we spent our time taking up two floor boards until, after about an hour, we thought it was time to ask the girl for a pail, as we had caught two rats and wanted something to put them in.

Now we had to make an appearance of busy-ness, for we knew our employer would not return before six, and we wanted to be there when he came, for we wanted to be paid, having come out with empty pockets and no lunch.

By the time he came in there were five rats in the pail, and he paid us without demur, telling us to come again, and go through the house as we had suggested: which we said we should be only too glad to do. We hurried round to buy fried fish and potatoes, and suppers for those at home.

On the next visit there were seven rats hidden about our persons, and one by one they were added to the bucket during the course of the day. When the master came home that night, and saw seven big rats all dead and lying huddled in the pail, he turned to brother Bill and exclaimed, 'Seven big rats! Seven and five make twelve – all in one private dwelling! I would not have believed it, but I have seen it with my own eyes.' We felt no shame as he paid us, only that this was the rich feeding the poor, for we were well aware that he could afford all we might ask.

We should have company next day we were told, for the son of the house would like to see us at work. We knew him already, had nick-named him Harold Lloyd after the film star of that name, for he wore a pair of thick-rimmed glasses just like the star's.

We came prepared – but not with dead rats this time; under Bill's shirt, and kept in place with a good thick waistcoat, was a live rat, and a big one. Bill didn't mind rats anywhere: it would not have been the first time he had won a bet over them. He would go into a pub, bet anyone present that he would put a live rat inside his shirt, be tied up at sleeves and waist so there should be no escape, and then slip a ferret in after, to kill within the shirt. And there he would stand, with arms above his head, while the rat squealed and the ferret hung on and they raced around his body – and the onlookers watched with horror as the shirt stained redder and redder; and then Bill would take out the ferret with the rat, and the rat was dead. Good bets they laid and especially when the company had drunk well and was money-loose.

Harold Lloyd let us in himself, and led the way to the bedroom where we had been working, and where the boards were still up because we felt the work had not been completed. We knew what the work was to be, but we didn't see how we were to manage it, with the lights bright in the room. 'Rats will never come out while the room's as light as this, we'll have to turn down the gas jets,' I said to Harold, and before he could answer, I had done it.

Bill and I knelt down together over the gaping boards, and I took a ferret from my pocket, and held it down with one hand, nudging Bill with the other elbow, to tell him to let the rat loose in the hole, that I might drop the ferret in behind it. We miscalculated. The moment the rat was free, it bolted, not into the darkness of the hole, but straight for Harold's legs. He let out a bellow, and I shouted, 'One out!'

What with the rat's coming for him, and the shout I gave, Harold dived for the door. Whether the rat actually touched his legs or not I couldn't see, but Harold lifted his legs high and went down the stairs by the banisters.

We were not far behind, for the rat too had made for the stairs, and we were making grabs at it. It reached the bottom, and so did we. All I could see of Harold was his head, peering out from a small opening of the front room door. Luckily, there was no hole for the rat to dive into, and as it scuttled along the bottom of the front door, Bill laid successful hold of it.

The door of the front room had slammed tight.

I winked at Bill holding the rat safely in his grasp, and tapped at the door. 'Open the door,' I called through, 'we've got the rat, it's quite all right.'

The door opened a crack, and three heads appeared there,

OF RATS AND RATTING

for the master had not gone out after all. 'There's nothing to be afraid of,' I said reassuringly. 'I'd like to show you why we charge so much for killing a rat.'

Their eyes went big with expectant horror. 'Put him down, Bill,' I ordered, 'and hold him till the ferret gets a bite.' 'No, don't shut the door, just wait till the ferret gets a grip.'

That ferret knew what to do, and while its muzzle sank into the fur of the rat's neck, and the red blood oozed out, I looked up, to see the spectators with hands at their own throats.

Our employer whispered, 'Did you see that, Mother? Did you see that?'

'You know, of course,' I put in, 'that if one of those rats so much as walked over your food, you might be poisoned?'

The best rat-catchers in London, that's what they said we were. We picked up the ferret and the dead rat, and went upstairs again, alone this time, for no one had any desire to watch more of our work. But we knew it was the end – all good things must come to it, the time had come to put back the floor boards and pack up our gear. I bent down beside the gap in the floor, and there inspiration came to me. 'Lend me the torch, Bill,' I said, 'I want to look in.' I was right, the joists ran right through to the far side of the next room: the only one we hadn't visited, the bedroom of the master and his wife. 'Put a string on the ferret,' I said, 'and let me have the dead rat!' Nobody, I knew, would want to see that any more. I gave the ferret the rat, and let him go into the next room, under the floor. I waited till he was well in, then watched with the torch till he should let go. In that second I had jerked him away and left the rat where I wanted it.

Now I could put the floorboards back with a light heart, for I knew there would be one more visit.

With gear in hand down we went, to tell how our ferret had killed under the floor of the next room, for we had heard the squeal of the rat. We thought we had better come once more and get it out, before it made unpleasantness in the room. We must certainly come, the master said, and now that he had seen a killing and got over it, he'd be happy to watch us at our work. You mustn't be too hard on us, if we had a good laugh when we were safely away from the house, to think how things had turned out all in our favour, and knowing full well that a rat was there, lying ready for us on the morrow.

We arrived in good time, complete with drill and saw, for the floorboard was one long run of board without a join, and we had no wish to take up the whole board.

'First,' I announced, 'we'll make a test with the ferret, just to find where the rat lies.' It didn't take long, for over the spot where I knew it to be I dipped down the nose of the ferret and he sniffed eagerly, as I declared, 'It lies just about here!'

We drilled the holes to let in the saw, and took up a length of board. Bill gripped the ferret and pushed it in, waiting till it took hold, then out came the rat; looking huge even though dead and cold.

Our employer's wife had come up as well and stood beside her husband – and a rare treat it was to see the smiles of happiness on their two faces. They might have to pay for it, but at least they were given satisfaction. 'That,' declared Mother, 'is the rat that went "Clomp, Clomp!" over mine head!'

We were praised again, and so delighted was our employer that he sent us down to his sister's house to see if she had rats, for they had been hearing noises.

When I came back, and reported to him quite truthfully, that it was only mice, you could read the pleasure in his face. He drew out his wallet, and handed me two pound notes, one each for the finest rat-catchers in town.

On Taking Pheasants

Now I would tell you more of the man who sold me the long net for catching rabbits which proved to be ten feet short. Lammie Squires was his name, and for all he tricked me over the net, he was a good man and a good poacher. When I knew him, he was getting old, and he had crawled about so much in the damp undergrowth and crouched so long upon the moist earth his knees were thickened and stiffened with rheumatism, so that he would never run again. He came to cutting up pieces of carpet to make covers for his knees, and finding that they were soon soaked with the wet grasses, he begged some old inner tubes of cars and made knee-pads from those. He had been a lone wolf all his days, never marrying, and never taking anyone into his confidence. It was long after we had first become firm friends that he asked me to go with him, feeling perhaps that I was a man after his own heart, or perhaps that the burden of his traps and snares was more than his old shoulders cared to carry. I certainly shared in the carrying, but I shared in the takings too: and a fine honest man Lammie proved to be in the sharing. Half, he said, was to be mine, and half was put for me at the end.

Lammie thought nothing of going off into the woods for a week, living there without setting foot beyond, like a wild creature himself. He could move with no more noise than a cat, and taught me too to go in silence. 'I'm a quiet man, myself,' he would say, 'and being always alone, I knew if I heard a strange sound, or a step, that someone else was in the woods with me, and I took precautions. When there are two of you, you can never be quite sure; and you can't afford to make mistakes.'

Then one day, and a proud day it was for me, Lammie said, quietly, 'Alf, I know where there's a lovely lot of pheasants. Can you make time to come with me for four or five days?' I said I could. 'We shall have to go carefully,' Lammie cautioned, 'for they're on Dedman's Estate – and Dedman's on the Bench; it won't do to be caught.'

We went to Hoddesdon, and thence made our way, unseen, to the wood where we were to take the pheasants. But first, Lammie took me to a haystack in the corner of a field, and there we hid our gear, for, as he said, we didn't want to carry that round with us.

Then we moved into the wood itself, for Lammie must look for the best place to work. He knew within a little where the pheasants were, now he wanted to see where they would come – at his invitation. His idea was to build a hedge or fence, just high enough to stop the pheasants going over it, but with gaps through which they would go; and in each gap he would place a snare, tied to a branch of tree pulled down and ready to swing aloft with the pheasant. An idea simple in itself, but calling for the knowledge of years to know just where to work and how to make the preparations.

We did nothing more the first day, then cooked a little meal and sat talking quietly as dusk came into the woods, and the pheasants started to call, little guessing what a joyous sound it was to us.

These were the times when Lammie told of the things he had learnt in his poaching life. I listened gratefully, for no poacher, however old he is, or how successful, has ever finished learning.

'Never take your ferret and nets with you on a frosty morning,' said Lammie, crouching there beside me, 'you'll draw a blank if you do. With the ground hard with frost, every step will ring in the hollow earth of the buries like a bell and warn the rabbits. Even if you take off your boots and creep up barefoot, you can't use nets, for you can't drive the pegs in without noise. Creep up, put your ferret in, and wait with the gun. And I'll tell you something on that, too; if a bolted rabbit is shot at and not killed, often it will make for a strange bury, and go in and there suffer death from a ferret rather than bolt again.'

There was a long pause while Lammie saw again the frightened rabbit, eyes big in its head, streaking for safety, and he knowing just how to take it when the time came. 'I've been out,' he went on quietly, 'most of my life, almost always alone. I've had the time to watch and to listen, and I've learned things. I'll tell you something I wouldn't tell to many – not they, they'd only laugh – but I tell you, I can hear the rabbits talking one to the other – and I know what they're saying.'

I didn't laugh. I had heard rabbits in the hutch communing together, why should not Lammie have heard too, and with infinite patience, and observation, and endless hours of living close to them, have learned to understand? I believed him implicitly.

Next morning after we had eaten breakfast, with the sun just edging a little ray of warmth into the wood, Lammie set me to work cutting twigs about eighteen inches long, and sharpening one end to a point with my knife. Every chip that flew from my blade, every white splinter of wood, I must pick up: if but one was left in the grass to catch the eye of keeper or passer-by, we should have had all our labour for nothing.

OF RATS AND RATTING

As I cut, and the pile of little stakes grew, he set to work on his hedge, criss-crossing the twigs, putting back the grasses and the vegetation so that nothing showed; and so he worked his way, twenty yards or more, through the wood. But as I have said, that hedge or fence was not solid. Every two or three feet, whenever a branch hung conveniently overhead and within Lammie's reach, Lammie left a gap, big enough for a pheasant to go through. Now I saw the skill that had chosen the route the fence must follow.

When it was finished, Lammie declared it was a good job we had done.

'Now,' he went on, 'we must make a little trip to the haystack, for I want something for those pheasants tonight.' From the top layers of the stack he took some paper bundles. 'You get some blackberries on the way back,' he said, 'pheasants are very fond of a blackberry, and they won't mind if they're still red.'

Together we went along the fence once more, and in each gap Lammie placed some food – pheasant food: a few raisins, a sprinkle of corn, and some of my blackberries. There was more food too, each side of the gap, some six inches away, so that from whichever side the pheasant came, there was something to lead him on, and into the gap, and through. We wanted those birds to feel free to feed, and indeed they were free to all there was for the present.

We spent another night in the woods, and with the morning light Lammie took me to see what had happened. Into each gap he looked with keen appraisal, and very delighted he seemed with what he found. At the end of the fence, he said, 'Alf, you get some more blackberries, I'm going to feed them again tonight, and then, the next night, we shall take the lot.'

All day we lay quiet in the woods, never far away, so that if by bad chance anyone should discover our work, we should know, and not be caught.

Lammie was filled with a quiet joy, for the food had gone again. 'Tonight,' he told me, 'we shall give them all the provisions we have left, so you be sure the blackberries are ready!'

With the chill that came with the going of the sun, we had

done all we could. At every gap a branch hung down, held lightly under a notch on another twig pushed into the ground, and to each branch was tied a wire noose, for in those days we used the plain noose that ran up tight and killed at once: and every noose was held in place with a twig, ready for the head of a pheasant to run in.

We went to our thicket to sleep, a short sleep broken by the call of foxes, making us hope they were not after our precious pheasants: but a sleep that refreshed.

We were finally awake as the birds are, before the first true light. But we did not go straight to our fence. Instead Lammie told me to pick up a stick and go softly to the outside of the wood. 'And take a good look about you,' he warned, 'before you make a sound. Then work back through the wood, zigzagging as you come, to the fence, and beat the thickets, making all the commotion you can. The pheasants won't worry, not if they're where they should be by now, but there'll likely be a rabbit or two still out, skulking in the thickets, and a gap or two in the fence with no pheasant taken. We might as well take all we can get.'

He went off himself to the far side of the wood, and a fine time we had of it, making as much noise as we could with our feet and our sticks, after all the hours of enforced silence.

And sure enough, when we came to our fence, there were the pheasants, red and gold above our heads, and among them a rabbit or two, still limp and warm. We set to, cutting down all we had got, and then we destroyed the fence, for it was no use to us now. There would be few pheasants left alive in that piece of wood, and every hour the fence remained it was a source of potential danger. So we took the stakes away, and some we hid in the thickets, and the rest we threw into a little stream. The pheasants we hid under the haystack, with the rabbits, coming and going always by a different route so as to leave no tell-tale path.

Then we returned to the stream, and washed for the first time in days. We straightened out our clothing and made ourselves as presentable as we could, remembering that we had not shaved for days.

It was time for home; and we set off, returning with empty

OF RATS AND RATTING

hands. There, we shaved, and put on what good clothes we might have, even if it were only a collar and tie. Then, around dinner-time, when all good folk were thinking of dinner and were getting within doors, we set forth again, Lammie and I, each carrying from home a carpet bag for tools, and with a tool or two showing for all the world to see. Back at the haystack we filled those bags with all they would carry, and with the tools still showing to prove what respectable artisans we were, we set off for home once more, and not a breath of suspicion about us. I went with Lammie again, after, to different woods, and many a pheasant has walked unknowing home, in that carpet bag, and so to the tables of those who know good food when they see it.

Snaring called for skill, and specialist knowledge of the art. But there are more ways of taking pheasants than with a snare and I think that of them all I was happiest when going through the woods with a gun, for shooting was a skill I had been brought up to, and all I saw I might kill and get away with in one night. Ours was never the wholesale robbery you hear of today, when gangster toughs arrive by lorry or car ready to beat up any keeper man enough to tackle them, and then destroy with a battery of fire-arms all his care and work of a year, and are off and away before help can arrive. We shot what we saw, certainly, but we never cleared the coverts and we ran always the risk of being caught.

When the pigeons broke in their flight, and wheeled and fluttered and dropped into the trees to roost, we were in the woods watching the golden dusk, waiting for the signal – the 'Cock-up!' 'Cock-up!' of pheasants going up to sleep.

There was little we needed to carry with us, a ·410 gun, a pocketful of cartridges, and a lump of whitening, the sort that was used by everybody then to whiten the hearth, a penny a lump.

When day had fallen into silence, so still that a man dare hardly speak his own thoughts for fear of the sound of his voice, we set off, a mile, two miles, through the woods, without a light of any kind save what the night gave us, and we sought out our pheasants. We peered into the boughs till we made out the dark blob that was pheasant and then on that tree we made a large cross with our whitening, facing so that we should see it on our return.

For minutes on end, for half an hour, an hour, I peered into the lacing of the boughs, seeing nothing but the grey of the sky behind, and the interweaving branches, and blobs that were pheasants. I made the cross on the tree, seeing it still interlaced with tracery of boughs. I went to the next tree, and peering up saw the same boughs I had seen before, and before that, and all evening. I looked down, and around me at the night; branches, branches everywhere and light sky between them: I was blind, with the wood-blindness known only to poachers and keepers.

I crouched where I was, there on the earth, and buried head in hands, waiting for sight to return: and Bill, for two of you are needed on this job and it was usually brother Bill who came, waited there beside me gun resting lightly in his arm, ears alert for the first warning sound.

And at last, the blindness passed away, and the trees came back in their own form, and we went on to the end of the wood. There we might rest till day was near, for the pheasants would wait. They might rise as we stood below, to crane over to peer down at our stealthiness, but they would not fly, for the pheasant is loth to leave a chosen roost. Never a shot had we fired, not a soul had we seen, but now we must shoot; 2 a.m. and time to begin. If there was a road near by, we stole out to it for one last precaution – to lay head to road and listen for the step of keeper, or of village constable on his lonely beat. A mile away you may hear them, with the road hard and the night still. Convinced that all was clear, we stole into the woods again for the journey back.

The marks on the trees shone white and plain, the gun with its little two-and-a-half-inch cartridge made no more noise than the crack of a twig underfoot: and as one of us shot, the other pounced on the fallen bird in case it might be a runner. And so from tree to tree, travelling all the time towards home; every pheasant so many score yards nearer. If now constable or wakeful keeper should hear a shot, and wait for the next to be certain of its direction, he would be hard put to tell it, for each would sound from a different quarter.

And so at last we were back; and there we put on our coats, raglan coats, loose fitting especially at the sleeves, and a good camouflage. Under the coats were the pheasants, tied by their necks, in fours or fives, hanging under the arms of the coats, and nobody any the wiser, save by mischance.

Too early yet, for the first tram or train, or bus; we might make up some of the sleep we had earned, and missed. We got down behind hedge or fence, and waited – always for the second bus or train, just in case someone was on the look-out for characters going by first bus into town. No sooner did we hear the sound of the engine on the bright air, or see the bus coming over the brow of a hill, than we were through the hedge and waiting.

On the train there was always an empty compartment: by bus we took the rear seat if possible, that none might see behind us, and there we arranged ourselves comfortably, with the weight of the birds on the seat: and so we chatted of the day ahead, and of our daily work, knowing that the conductor would see only two honest workmen setting off.

Of Fish and Fishing

As the birds of the air and the beasts of the field were the meat that came to our table, so the fish that varied our meals we took from stream and reservoir, at times from other sources.

When we could get it we fished with permission, more often we poached. From the days of Father's willow rod and my own bamboo I progressed till I came to fashioning rods of my own, with the weights and the floats to go with them. I would make my own hooks, following Father's practice. I remembered how he would take a piece of stiff wire, sharpen an end to a point, temper it in a flame, hammer it flat it near the tip and shape off a barb, then bend the point round; and with those home-made hooks and the coarse lines we had, he brought home good fish. But any of the good fish of yesterday are outweighed by those caught today, when the balance is weighted in favour of the fisherman, with his splendid winches, his nylon lines, and unbreakable rods of feather weight; yet we, who learned our skills the hard way, can take dinner and supper from the grey water while others sit beside us with scarce a bite.

Three rules make for good fishing: learn the waters that you fish; find out the habits of the fish you hope to catch; know the bait that will catch them.

Often the bait that will catch big fish is the small fry of their own kind. Myriads of baby fish never live to grow up. We see it even in the aquarium at home. One day the water is glinting with tiny silver fish, the next there is hardly one to be seen, they have been eaten by their own kind, as I have found eel within eel, pike within pike, perch within perch and small roach inside large roach.

Our table fish were most often pike or perch taken with a small live roach or perch, held with a No. 6 hook. People will tell you that you must cut off the dorsal fin from a perch before you use it as bait, that no fish will swallow such an armoury of spikes. But we used our bait as the fish is used to seeing it, whole, and it was swallowed whole, head first, without hesitation. Many and many a score of fish I have taken with that bait.

We were never without it, for in the times of plenty we took all we needed and some over that would be used dead, preserved in formaldehyde, in the days when small fry were not to be had. We took these fish in hundreds from the reservoirs, poaching, as the same waters are poached today and always will be as long as there are men and fish.

For bait-catching brother Bill came with me, and changed into the old trousers and shirt we kept hidden in the hedge. They might be damp, they were soon to be damper. We would get on the bank above the reservoir, one eye ready for the first glimpse of a patrol on his rounds, the other on the surface of the water watching for the flash and glint of small fry leaping in terror from the perch or pike below. As soon as we saw that, we made ready. We waited for them to come in, small roach and small perch, a whole school of them, and behind, the big perch preying on their own. At times the big ones would come so fast they would rush right out of the water and on to the sloping concrete side – and there we grabbed them in haste, before they could struggle back.

When the small fish had swum into the corner where we were, Bill slipped into the water trailing a net alongside him, whilst I held the other end. He swam across the angle, clambered out and drew the net round back to me, and together we pulled it up, and a splendid haul we would make. We could sit back, bait-can beside us, and fish all day and still have some for pickling when we reached home.

We had two rods apiece, one lying on the bank beside us in

readiness, the other cast out. Every twenty or thirty minutes the small fry would come, leaping out to tell us that dinner was down below them, our dinner. We watched the float, struck as it went under, and laid the rod on the bank, for that fish was safely hooked. Now with the second rod, baited with a dead fish, or a silver spoon, or even a piece of silver paper, we cast again into the midst of the boiling water and caught another fish. At times we used to sink and draw, using dead bait, drawing it in and twiddling the line with our fingers to make it seem alive. Cast out some thirty yards, the heavy weight would take it into the depths, and we would draw in five feet, and another five feet, to lure the pike; for perch or pike will rush to snatch at a fish that seems damaged or out of sorts. Here is one of the surest ways of catching when big fish lie in deep water. Where the weeds are growing thick and the power of the water presses greenly through, stand quietly without movement, and after a time you will see a flop, flop, by the weeds. Drop the bait in, small roach or perch, or even a stickleback, and let the current carry it under the green weeds, and down goes your float with a tug.

We have taken pike by other means, with a noose of wire like a rabbit snare, slipping it without touch over head and shoulders as the fish lay motionless on the surface. We have taken them with snap tackle, using six hooks and striking at the first bite. There are other old methods now out of use, like the gorge bait method, illegal today, where a hook was embedded under the skin of a live fish, with the line coming out by the dorsal fin, and the hook lying point down beside the gill, a deadly and a cruel lure.

Today, prizes are regularly offered for the biggest catch, with strict rules and regulations, strictly enforced; and the fish caught are returned to the water to live again. We caught for food, having no urge to catch merely to throw back. Not from sentiment: though people will tell that it is cruel to take a fish with a hook. If it is so, then the clubs of today every week inflict incalculable cruelty upon the denizens of our waters. Yet I tell you that I have caught a fish ten minutes after my brother Syd had lost it, taken his hook from its mouth and handed it back. If a hooked fish is in agony, then it inflicts upon itself far greater torture in its struggle to be free, and should shun a hook for ever. And I have seen a pike taken with twenty-seven hooks embedded in it! No, we had no sentiment over hooks, we were out to catch food. In the same way, if we entered a contest, it was not so much for the sport of the game; we went in to win.

Winning a Competition

Bill and Syd were in a contest on the River Lee in the days before competitors were allotted a swim, a stretch of river to themselves, but had the right to fish from lock to lock.

They had taken their place well away from the rest, with the reservoir at their back on the other side of the fence. I was on the reservoir; I had been there since early day catching fish. Some for dinner, one for the competition, which was timed to begin at eight. I gave the competitors plenty of time to become absorbed, lying on my back unseen in the grasses and feeling how good it was to be here away from all the worries of the world, and with a fat perch waiting in the tin beside me.

As the sun grew hot I crawled through the grass to where my brothers should be, looked through the fence, and there was Bill, well aware of what I was hoping to do for him. 'Bill, Bill,' I whispered, 'I've got one, a big perch. Lay your rod across and I'll put him on.' Bill laid the rod across the grass within reach of the fence, and while he pretended to fumble about in his bag, I took the perch from the can and hooked it on. Before it knew what was happening that fish was swimming about in the River Lee, at the end of Bill's line. 'Don't land it,' I whispered urgently, 'till you've got a crowd round.' I crawled on down the fence, saw Syd sitting there alone and called to him, 'Bill's got a perch!'

Syd understood perfectly. I saw him lift his rod, and cast out again delicately, for of us all, Syd is the fisherman. After a moment he looked up, glanced across at Bill, laid his rod on the bank and stood up. 'Bill's got one. Bill's got a good'un!' he cried, and started off up the bank. I saw other rods being laid down, and other men coming, for if a Curtis was landing a good fish, it was likely to prove the fish of the day.

Oblivious to them all, Bill sat calmly playing his perch

till at last it was landed, and lay flapping in the grass, gills lifting and shutting. 'What a beauty!' someone cried. 'A pound and a half that is.'

And so it proved, and though we have taken from the reservoir many a heavier perch, it was good enough to win the contest, with a share of the prize money for me.

We were not the only ones to make sure of winning.

I was paid a visit one night by a member of a large fishing club. 'Alf,' he said, 'there's a little job you can do for me if you will, and I'll make it worth your while.'

He wanted two big roach, and I agreed to get them, which I did, from the reservoir, and was paid ten shillings for them. 'They'll do me splendidly,' the man said. 'I want them for the competition in a fortnight's time.'

I wished him luck. I didn't ask how he thought he was going to keep them in good condition for that length of time. I knew those roach would want fresh running water if they were to be fit for contest. He evidently knew too, as I discovered later, for he put those fish into the tank under the roof where the flushing of the cistern renewed the water, and kept them alive and well and won his prize.

That was years ago, but even today, when all is supposed to be done for the sake of the sport, there are those who cannot resist the prize. I recall a giant bream found floating and near to death, that was taken, weighed and photographed, and that won a handsome award, and was never heard of again, the fisherman being only too glad to get it quickly out of view.

Big Fish

Wandering in the fields as we did, it would have been strange had we cast no eye towards the streams that kept us company, and of course we did. We came to know them, to overcome their difficulties.

I know a hidden obstacle below water, that has taken many a fisherman's hook. I have been out at low water and collected them, and lost others of my own till I hit upon a plan. I took home the hooks, and heated them till they had lost much of their spring. Now if they were caught up, I gave a tug, they straightened out and I pulled them free. A moment's

OF FISH AND FISHING

work with a pair of pliers and they were in shape again, and good for holding a fish, for a fish properly hooked is held in the strongest part, the curve of the hook.

On the reservoirs it was a different kind of obstacle we had to circumvent, the patrol. Not that we were often caught red-handed, for unless we became too engrossed in our fishing we could see him coming long before. The moment we saw him we packed our tackle in haste, got over the Water Board fence, lay in the grasses and watched through the railings for him to pass. Sometimes we waited in vain. He had seen us too, and was seated in our fishing spot, waiting for us to return. After twenty minutes of idleness, we left our gear, went down the fence some two hundred yards, climbed back on to the reservoir, and wormed our way down the far side of the bank till we could see him sitting waiting, knowing that if he did happen to look up and see us, we would have ample time to make our escape.

They were good times, full of the joy of the risk of being caught, and poachers though we were, we bore no ill will towards the patrol; he left us alone long enough for us to take all we wanted; no man can effectively guard even one reservoir.

Others would have liked to be with us to learn our fishing spots, for a reservoir like any other lake has its times and its places; but we kept our knowledge to ourselves, and keep it to this day. Even strangers hoped to learn of a good thing when they saw our catch.

I was standing with Bill and Syd, waiting for a train among a crowd of fishermen all homeward bound, and all of course talking of the day's events.

Syd had his fish wrapped in cloth in a basket. One of a group looked down and said, 'Any luck, mate?'

'Caught a few perch,' said Syd, knowing they were fine fish. 'May I have a look?'

Syd took off the cloth and showed him. What excitement there was! 'Abe, Abe, what fish!' the man cried. 'Come and have a look!' More gathered round, a party of Jews, all wanting to know what he used to catch them, and what he wanted for them.

Then Abe drew Syd a little to one side, and slipped a coin

into his hand. 'Here, have a drink,' he said, 'and now, where did you get them?'

Syd dropped his voice so that the others should not overhear. 'You know the old barges along the Lee,' he said, pointing vaguely out, 'take the last barge, fish off the end of that, and you'll cane them right enough.'

Abe called to his friend, and whispered the good news to him. 'No work tomorrow! Down by the end barge on the Lee!'

How they got on we do not know, we were back on the reservoir, the King George V at Chingford, not then open for fishing.

Wartime Fishing

Perhaps our finest time on that reservoir came with the Second World War, for then we poached with permission. I had been close enough to it to see that the banks were stationed with guns and armed soldiers, and if all were not real, at least there were enough to make me feel that this was the end of my poaching there.

Then I learned that some of the soldiers were in the habit of going into a little pub well known to me. I made it my business to meet them there. Of course, we got to talking of fishing, and they told me how much they would like to while away a few hours at the sport, but they had no hooks or lines. They were not easy to get in those days, but I had a fair stock in hand for the little trade I had in fishing tackle. I knew I had enough to help them out, but I wanted to be there too. In the end they suggested that I should go and see their Captain, a keen fisherman himself, and see what we could do between us.

Of course I made time to go, and the upshot was that I left seven rods with him for the men to use, as I said, to catch a few fish and pass the time away when they were not on duty.

Best of all, as I was leaving the Captain said, 'Any time, Curtis, that you or your brothers want to come fishing you'll find a couple of uniforms hanging up at the back of the huts.'

He was as good as his word, and many a time we gave the patrol a smart salute as he approached. 'Caught any?' he'd

OF FISH AND FISHING

inquire as he passed. Caught any? I should think we did, with only ourselves and the soldiers, and the whole reservoir to fish in.

Many of my catches went into the factory of Messrs. Lebus, a great factory where I had charge of the repair and maintenance of the tool makers' machines. There I sold the fish, usually to Jews, for they were anxious to get hold of freshwater fish and paid well for them. Many a day has begun with my going to the bench to find half a dozen men waiting to see what I had brought.

One morning I turned up at the gate with something in a sack, and had of course to declare it before I was allowed through. 'Two fish,' I announced, 'two big ones.' And they were. The night before I had taken my rod from the cupboard where I kept my tools and a spare rod, and getting on to the reservoir just outside the works, I had fished the Cut, where some fine fish had their station. I took a pike, a twenty-six pounder, hid it up a pipe, walked along the Cut and came back along the opposite bank. And here, right where I had caught the first, I landed a second pike, just half a pound heavier. These were the fish in my sack.

The news had soon spread. No sooner had I shown one man at the bench than men started coming from all over the works. All my pleadings to them to go away, 'You'll have the guv'nor in', were of no avail.

The foreman came over to see what I had this time.

'I've got two extraordinary fish,' I said, 'might be twins.'

He took a quick look. 'Well, get the men away from the bench,' he said, 'you'll be getting me transferred.'

As he was talking who should walk in but Mr. Lebus himself, a man well-nigh a millionaire, one we all admired, for he took his place in the bus queue with the rest of us instead of using petrol in a big car.

He called to the foreman to know what all the men were doing round Curtis's bench. The foreman explained that I had two large fish. Mr. Lebus came over to see for himself. 'Show me,' he commanded, 'the fish that all this commotion's about.' The men stood back for him to see. He gazed down in astonishment. 'You caught these?'

'Yes, sir.'

'Where?'

'No names, no pack drill, sir!' I said, using the popular expression of the day. He smiled, and walked away.

The next thing I knew, the foreman wanted to see me. 'Put those fish out on a table in one of the dug-outs,' he said – meaning in one of the air-raid shelters with which we were provided.

So I displayed them, on white paper, and was told I might go round the shops and tell the men that any wishing to view the fish might come along. Many were only too pleased to have a break, and in they came. By midday those two fish had made me five pounds, they had gone to the highest bidder, for money was easy to make in the jobs we had. But best of all, I had not been dismissed for taking the men from their work; that was the sort of man our employer was.

As I was leaving at the end of the day one of the purchasers said, 'I'll show you how to cook that fish, Curtis.' Sure enough he did; he brought me half a dozen dainty sandwiches filled with a savoury made of the liver of the pike. I shared the sandwiches out, and we all agreed that though we could put no real name to its taste, we had never had anything so delicious.

I tried hard and often to obtain the recipe for such a delicacy, but promises were all I ever got.

Many a night, while I worked at Lebus's, I have waited till I had seen the Water Board patrol go off at six o'clock, then climbed the fence and made off along the reservoir, with every step I took along its bank a step towards home. I fished with a spoon, a big kidney-shaped affair six inches long by half as broad, made from the outer casing from an old teapot; one of the most successful baits I ever made. Even with my old-fashioned wooden winch, it sailed well out into the reservoir, to come back with a slow and steady twist, and many a pike it has lured to its end.

Small Fish

There came the time when we found that a thriving trade in live bait might be had with the dealers. Now our knowledge of rivers and streams proved invaluable. First, I prepared the nets, different nets for different tasks.

One we had for river fishing; a big affair of mutton cloths sewn together, with weights to sink it, and corks to hold up the top, and a large hole at each side near the top to let the water escape, or neither the net nor ourselves could have held the weight.

It was better worked with two people, but if I was alone, I used a stake to hold the near side of the net, pegging it down below the shallows where the ripples told of the gravel below, and where the fish lay, facing the stream. Now, in my old clothes, I waded across, let the net fill out so that the bag in its middle was open for the taking of the fish, then waded back, bringing the net in a great sweep right to where I had begun. I pulled it up, threw out any fish too big for bait, and put the rest into the cans.

This was really a net for two, the second to walk the fish downstream into the bag and help with the lifting. There was another I made, a flue or bag net, which was thrown from the arm. Fastened to my waist were two strings, one from the top, the other from the bottom of the net. Two other strings there were, which I folded on top of the net as it lay in readiness looped upon my arm. With the ends of the strings in my hand. I turned my body away from the river, and swung back and threw the net out and across; pulled on the long strings in my hand, drew the net into a circle, and dragged it in.

It was hard work, it might take me a whole day to work half a dozen places, but every draw brought its prize. As I caught them I put the fish into sinkers – large tins with holes punched top, bottom and sides to let the water flow through and keep the fish breathing. Then, at the end of the day, I took the sinkers from the shallows, tied a long string to each, and sank them into deep water; there to wait for the time when I had bait-cans to fill for the shops. And the more shaken up they were, the more fish I found lived through the journey, perhaps by aeration of the water. Roach were always the first to die, for they need plenty of oxygen. Carp are long lived, and slow to die under adverse conditions. I have kept them alive seven hours, wrapped in wet cloth. I have found them still alive in ponds where summer heats had dried the water away, and almost all the carp had was one wet side. At home in the yard of the cottage, where the ground was always damp from the ditch beyond, and where there was a slight leak from the tank in which I kept fish alive, I came upon a carp that had evidently been dropped and had flapped under the tank out of sight. It was still alive days after, with that little trickle on the damp ground. I have brought home a large tench, caught in the Cambridge Ouse and wrapped in wet cloth, all the way back to Edmonton, filled a bath, put it in, and had it full of vigour next day. A wrapping of wet grass is often sufficient to keep a fish alive through a journey, and many a perch I have brought home in the bag has lifted tail and flapped on the kitchen table an hour or so after its catching.

As the rivers and the man-made lakes helped to feed our families, so we took toll of the ponds in their turn. One of them lay at the top of Green Dragon Lane at Winchmore Hill. The pond was in the grounds of the A1 Milk Co., opposite the hospital, and when I first went there to fish I was careful to carry a bottle of A1 milk, that all might know me for a customer.

It was a big pond, though the fish I took from it were small: little carp, golden carp some five inches in length, which found a ready sale to aquarium keepers and for bait. From break of day to breakfast time at eight I sat fishing, and again in the evening. When it grew too dark to see the float, I put on the hook a white butterfly with clipped wings, and went on catching.

On the site stood a gipsy caravan and the man kept an eye on the grounds, and the happenings thereon. I knew him well by sight, and it was only a matter of time before we became acquainted. He stopped me one day to ask if I knew anyone with a ferret they would be willing to lend him for a few days; for he meant to catch some of the rabbits that ran about the fields. I said I would lend him one if he would take care of it. 'I'll do that,' he said, 'and now – you come here fishing quite a bit – would you like some fish?'

He took me over to his caravan, and there behind it showed me two old baths, overcrowded. I said I'd bring the ferret

OF FISH AND FISHING

next morning, and I did, going along with Bill to help carry home the fish.

'Where d'you get them all?' Bill asked, staring at the baths.

'Scooped them out of the ditches. They let the water down from higher up, and it swept through the pond and flooded the ditches, and brought the fish with it. The waters have run away, except in the pools, and there's plenty of fish in those now, under the overhanging brambles.' We thanked him, and told him we'd certainly look. As soon as the baths had been cleared of their fish, we kept our word. We took a scoop with a handkerchief across the first pool, and that was sufficient. We were there next morning with a net or two of our own make and the bait-can. There was no fishing to do, we just took fish out, and put them into the can – four to five hundred in a can. Then back we went to The Green at Edmonton, to Mr. Lingwood, whose shop is there to this day. Twelve shillings and threepence a hundred he was willing to give us, and twice in the day we made that twenty-five minute run by cycle; for it was good money, ready money; but too good to last.

When the pools were empty I went back to fishing the pond, sometimes alone, sometimes with Bill. One morning when we were there together Bill whispered, 'Cops! Three coming this way. I wonder if it's about all those carp?'

'Get on fishing!' I said.

The policemen came up quietly behind us, then one of them circled Bill to get a good look at his face, then looked at me. 'It's all right,' he said, 'he's not here!' He turned towards us again. 'Been fishing long?'

'Since daybreak.'

'Seen anything floating?'

'Floating, what d'you mean?'

'A body!' We hadn't. He gave a sigh of relief. 'That's one job I'm not sorry to lose.' Then he explained. One of the patients from the hospital had escaped, and it was feared might be drowned.

'Bill,' I said, 'these gentlemen are thirsty: fetch a couple of quarts over.' Bill went off, only too glad to be out of that company. We sat and talked of fishing.

'You after little fish like those?' one of the policemen asked, peering into the can. 'I know where there's plenty of those.' I thought he was going to tell of the carp in the ditches. 'D'you know the greenhouses?' he went on. 'There's a sump with water for the greenhouses, full of fish. As they're taken up they're put into a big water butt near by.'

Bill returned with the ale, we quenched our thirst, the policemen got up, wished us luck, and went. Luck? They had put it in our way. 'Listen, Bill,' I said, as they disappeared, 'we're not going home till evening. I've just heard of some fish.' I told him the tale.

We rested that day, waiting for evening. It was nothing for us to miss a meal or two, and neither we nor those at home would worry on that score. About tea-time we moved to watch proceedings at the greenhouses. We saw a man take a last look round, then set off for home. Our bait-can we had already emptied into one of the ditch pools; now we set off under shelter of the hedges, climbed the wooden palings, and were inside the nursery.

'You keep a look-out,' I said, 'while I see what's in the butt.' It didn't take long to find it, and a bucket standing alongside. I drew a pailful, and hurried back to Bill.

'Give me the can, and get back over the fence – we'll put them all into the pools; we can't take them all in one night.'

We worked hard: and when I could reach no more I tipped the butt over, and scrabbled the fish from the ground.

'That's the lot,' I announced, as I handed them over to Bill. 'I've pushed the butt over.'

'You've spoilt us for the sump then! They'll know that someone's been, and keep a watch. Just let me get rid of these.'

'I'll come over with you,' Bill said on return. And together, with the help of the bucket, we filled the butt again and put in a few fish, knowing that if anybody wondered at the state of the ground in the morning, they probably would not give it a second thought.

On the first night of moon we were there again, with a home-made net large enough to drag the sump. The first haul was so heavy with fish we could not lift it. All night we worked, taking the fish from the sump and carrying them to the ditches, where they were safely trapped in the pools till we should want them; more than a good week's fishing in a single night.

The gipsy was outside his caravan as we passed in the grey morning, and he waved us over, to tell us what a good ferret I had lent him, and to ask if I would be willing to part with it. I was so delighted with the way things had turned out, I told him to keep it, and made a firm friend, one who kept us informed of all that went on around the pond, even to the ducks that came with the onset of winter.

So it was that one evening I stood with a gun under a tree on the bank – and did not shoot; for the ducks came in down the centre of the pond, out of range. There was a tree opposite on the far bank, but just as far from the ducks. The next time I went with Syd, and placed him under one of the trees, while I stood under the other. The ducks came in as usual, down the middle of the pond. Syd stepped out, waved his arms, shouted. They swerved, came within reach, and – bang! bang! – there was one each for us.

You may think our lives were selfish and rewards easy, but often we lived the hard way, with nothing much falling to the gun or being taken on the line. We were sportsmen too, though we fished for food. I have spent day after day for weeks trying to catch one barbel that was as clever as I – or nearly.

There were people who seemed determined to spoil our sport. Poacher as I was in those days, I might be caught for fishing illegally, yet still in my heart not see the wrong of it.

Fishing Tales

Syd and I are cross-line fishing. I throw him a line across the stream, tie to my side a five-foot catgut with a fly on it, and call to Syd to draw in the line, taking the fly to midstream. I touch it down lightly upon the water, and catch a dace. That is illegal, for two men are fishing with one line. But why? I may cast my line with a weight upon it as far as I like, tie my fly on again, and walk upstream till my fly is over the dace, and take as many as I can. That is legal. Why?

One day when I was fishing – cross-line fishing – in the old

River Lee, a voice behind me said, 'That's a good one you've caught, son.' The police!

'Yes,' I agreed, 'it's not a bad one.'

'That chap over there's got his line tangled with yours,' he went on. Then I knew he understood nothing of it.

'Oh, he's only holding the end of my line.'

'Go on, show me, I'd like to see you catch another.' It didn't take long: and as I stooped to take off the fish, I signed to Syd to peg down his end and make off.

'Would you like a go?'

'That I would,' said the policeman and sat down, swung his legs over the edge and put his helmet down beside him. He was soon engrossed, with the fly dancing to the surface and up again – so engrossed he didn't notice me slip off after Syd. And there we left him fishing illegally. Or was it illegal? To this day I do not know; but we enjoyed the thought, and all we had lost was a reel of cobbler's thread for a line, a few feet of gut, a hook and a fly – a live one, caught from the nearest patch of horse manure.

There are many tales I could tell of the Lee.

One day I was there with my family, getting used to the feel of a rod in my hands again, for I had only just left hospital after a third stay. Not far away a boy was fishing with his father. After a time Father said he would like a drink and would I keep an eye on the boy while he was gone?

I said I would. I was to remember that promise.

While the man was away, I caught a jack of about two pounds weight. 'Look at that little chap watching,' said Sally. 'Give it to him, Alf!'

'There you are, tell Father you caught it,' I said, as I put it down beside him. He looked up, speechless.

'That was a good thought of yours, Sally,' I told her as I sat down, and looked over to the boy to see his legs sticking out of the water, slowly sliding down the shelf.

I made a dash; so did Sally. 'You're not going in,' she cried. 'What about all these others?' She was thinking of the Thermogene I was still wearing after pleurisy.

But no one else had moved. 'Hold hands!' I cried, and the four of us made a chain. I went in up to my waist and, as I did so, the boy slipped again. I managed to hook a finger in the turn-up of a trouser leg – with twenty-eight feet of water below. I pulled steadily; he rose a little; I grabbed his legs and up he came, full of mud, his face invisible. We put our coats down for him, and worked for all we knew. We had got rid of the mud, and he was just showing signs of coming round, when his father returned.

I have no need to dwell upon his distress. His boy, he said, was subject to fits; any excitement might bring one on. He brought him out fishing to give him peace and quiet, with nothing to disturb him. He begged me to accept five shillings for all I had done. 'You take him straight away home,' I said, 'and buy him a tot of whisky on the way, instead.'

I have seen stark tragedy there too, in almost the same spot. It was a Sunday, and we were picnicking. A man sat with his wife and child not far away. The man began to change ready for swimming, for nobody minded there. Three or four minutes later the woman came running over to ask if we had seen her husband come up – he had taken a dive from the bank. We hadn't, and he didn't come up till the river was dragged, and they found him, drowned, caught under an old chain. Most people are afraid of weeds in the water, yet I have walked through weeds, swum among them, and even dug under water for lilies and been surrounded by weeds, and had no fear of them, and come to no harm through them. Our greatest worry, apart from the glass that people will throw in, was a little beetle. When we were in the water dragging, one of us would let out a yell, and drop the corner of the net. The bite of that beetle or whatever it was, seemed to **paralyse** us momentarily.

Death of a Fish

Even fish may meet with tragedy in water, in their own habitat.

I sit by a river, idling a sunny hour away in memories. The water flows by like silver without a ripple. A dragonfly comes and goes on dry restless wings. And then as he turns, my eyes catch a movement, a gentle motion on the far side. A branch of willow trails in the water; I watch it intently; yes, it is moving, slowly, softly upstream and back. The only movement in all that afternoon.

I go over the bridge to see. And there, in the water, snared, helpless, is a monster pike, made tremendous by its terrible thinness, doubling its real length; a backbone of fish, covered with skin. I draw it out, and lay it on the bank. From its mouth runs the line that in the pride of its strength it broke as it ran, and that it could have broken again and again, but the supple willow branch allowed no strain, and the fish was denied the tug that would have freed it. So the countryman, fishing for big eels, leaves his willow wand stuck into the mud of the bank, and all night the eel tugs, but is there in the morning held by the very weakness of the stick.

Of Divers Things Done

THE gun, the trap, the snare and the ferret, these were the tools of the poacher's art, together with the nets and a man's own skill and knowledge. Yet every poacher will tell how at times he makes a good haul using little beyond the chance Nature placed in his way.

There was the day Bill and I went to the big hollow I have told of, which appeared in Mr. McMullen's fields when the earth collapsed into an old chalk cutting. We were to net a big heading of holes that lay near the rim of the hollow, with an old stump of tree like a landmark in their midst. I remember that Mr. McMullen had gone off for the day to the races, waving us greeting as he went.

When we had found the rabbits' bolt hole, hidden in nettles, and had securely covered it and netted the rest, Bill slipped in the ferret, and I waited by, gun at the ready. But within a few minutes there came such a squealing from underground we knew there would be no shooting, the ferret had killed and was staying below with the rabbit.

I set off to the farm for a spade, for without the ferret we should achieve nothing. Coming back I thought I heard a voice, and creeping softly up, found Bill talking to a rabbit he held in one hand. 'Ah,' he was saying, 'I've half a mind to give you a run for it, but I won't, I have you safe now, and I'll give your liver something in the morning!' For rabbit liver and bacon was esteemed a great delicacy with us. Three rabbits Bill had taken while I had been away, that had run into the nets when I was certain we should catch none – but that was not to be the end of the tale.

When I asked him why he had been talking to himself, all Bill would say was, 'Look over there at Brinnie!'

Brinnie was sitting patiently by a small hole he had dug almost under the old stump.

'Never mind,' said Bill, 'let's get the ferret out first, and then we can see what he's got.'

Ten minutes' work with the spade, and we had reached the ferret and the rabbit it had killed. We put the rabbit with the others, and went over to Brinnie.

We threw ourselves down to peer into the small cavity – but it was our noses not our eyes that told us all we needed to know – for the bitter stench that came out of that hole could be made by nothing but rabbits, many rabbits, huddled close.

Bill scrabbled a hand in the hole, pushed in his arm, and brought out a live rabbit. One after the other they came up – to be swiftly dispatched. Upwards of a score of rabbits lay beside us on the turf: the turf they themselves had helped to make and to keep, as many a landowner found to his cost, when myxomatosis came to wipe out his rabbits.

We bent down to the empty hole, and felt around inside for explanation of such a chance; the hole was a block or blind hole with one entrance. All these rabbits must have run in at the killing by the ferret, to find their one means of exit blocked by the latest comers. But why? Why bolt all into one tunnel? And what was the hole anyway? For all we could ascertain it may have been no more than the hollow left by the rotting of a root from the old tree, but the rest is mystery to us to this day.

Bill on another occasion was out shooting when he saw the ears of a rabbit some forty yards away. He took a shot, saw the rabbit kick and jump, but stay where it was. He stole up to within twenty yards, and fired again. And going up he found the first shot had killed; bunny was in a snare and could not run. Such are the chances a poacher may find.

I will tell you a way to catch rabbits without gun, ferret or net. All a man needs is the chance to come on to the land a time or two, and then to be able to bide a favourable night.

He comes first in the dusk, when the sun is a red glow behind the wood, and waits for the rabbits to come out. He stands in the spinney above the little valley, and learns all he needs to know by keeping his eyes open – to learn the siting of the most populous warren. Then he may go home, with nothing done to scare a rabbit.

He comes next by day, borrows some hay from the rick, or gathers for himself a big bundle of dry grass, and hides it safely up in the hedge, for without that grass he is lost. Then, stepping softly, for it may be tonight that he will want to work, he goes from hole to hole, and places above each a piece of broken white crock brought for that purpose, or a light-coloured stone; so that he may know the holes again when he comes in the dark.

For that, he waits for a windy night, one with the leaves rattling and whistling, and then he must bring a friend, or a dog, for someone must go into the fields to drive the rabbits home.

He is in no hurry, but gives them plenty of time to travel well away from the bury, three fields away perhaps, instead of the mere fifteen yards they will venture on a wet night.

Between the hours of midnight and two of the morning he makes his final preparations, steals up to the holes, each marked with a glimmer of white, carrying with him his bundle of hay. He screws up tight handfuls, pushes a ball of hay down to arm's length in each hole, making sure it is jammed in tight.

Now the drive can begin. He waits by the holes, listening. There comes the thud and patter of quick feet returning in haste. The rabbits dash into the holes, one, perhaps two or three, in one hole, and now the work is fast and furious, and the haul good. And in the morning there is nothing left to tell the tale; for the holes look as they did before, with the crocks removed, and only a sack of rabbits the fewer.

I have caught rabbits by hand, for Brinnie would run them through a pipe that lay on the Sewage Farm, for me to gather them in my hands at the far end. And in the autumn, when the grasshoppers were living out the last of their days on the south side of the brambles, and the rabbits were lying out in the grassy spaces of the woods, I would go out, carrying a spade over my shoulder like a gun. Then, walking quietly, I would come upon a rabbit, squatting in dead grass almost the colour of its own jacket. Down in one sweep would come the spade, and the rabbit was mine.

We used as simple a trick for getting pheasants. You will recall the winter-warmers we had as boys. We used them now, to a different end. The tin with its smouldering rags, and its ventilation holes, had another hole now in its top, for taking the base of a collapsible blow tube. We would go into the woods, two of us together, about the time the pheasants were getting up to roost. Then with our tin smouldering, and the tube fitted, we were ready – with one addition, some flowers of sulphur sifted on to the rags. We lifted the blow tube till it was under the pheasant, then through a hole in its base we blew the noxious fumes around the bird, and it was not long before it tumbled from its perch stupefied.

Once I watched a poacher get a pheasant with no apparatus at all – but he was a fox.

I was sitting quietly in a wood not far from Hoddesdon, waiting in the hope of a free ferret, for I knew where several had gone to earth and stayed. The owls began to call from their roosting trees and fly across the deepening dusk. Then I was wide awake, for where nothing had been, a fox was standing, looking up into a tree. Pheasants! I sat without a move. The fox began to circle the tree, round and round without pause, till I began to wonder whether I was really seeing it. Then, as I watched, down from the tree tumbled a pheasant. There was a pounce, a flurry, and fox and pheasant went off together. I knew that foxes took pheasants at other times than nesting, for I had come across the bitten-off feathers that are the hall-mark of the fox, and I had wondered how. I had heard of their mesmerising the bird, but I would hesitate to call this mesmerising. The silly bird must have turned its head round and round to watch the fox below till it grew giddy and fell. That tale you may believe, for I saw it with my own eyes. I could tell other tales, less likely, that still have been believed by people in possession of their five senses.

There was the red-tailed rat. I first heard of it in a pub, where a man was talking loudly of the rat he had seen in his cellar, a rat with a red tail. I pricked up ears at this and edged over a little. I listened to him a while, for he seemed very much in earnest, then, 'Worth catching, that rat, eh, mister?'

'I'll give fifty shillings to anyone who can lay hands on it,' he declared, and I made up my mind to have that fifty shillings. Doughy the knife-grinder was there having a drink with me (not Doughy, my father, Doughy was a common nickname among our acquaintance) and as soon as he had finished, we went out together and hatched the plot. Doughy was to visit the Dust Shoot and there catch four rats and skin the tail off one, a thing easily done, for the tail peels readily.

The next day off we set, with three rats hidden in Doughy's shirt, and another with a red tail secreted somewhere about him.

We were shown the cellar where the sight had been seen. 'Don't forget, it's fifty shillings if you can catch it,' cried the excited owner. 'I must have it!'

'Don't you worry,' said Doughy, 'that rat's as good as caught.' Indeed it was.

'Let me know how you're getting on,' the man said, and up he went. We set to, pulling out boxes and the junk of years, making all the commotion we could, till we thought we must have made enough to impress him, and then we let the three rats go.

We gave them time to get among the boxes then up I went to invite the owner down to see for himself. 'You've rats right enough,' I told him. 'Come down and have a look, you can see them running about.' But come down he would not. All he wanted, he said, was that we should catch the rat with the red tail. So back I went, and we clattered about some more, till we decided it was time to produce what we had come for – and out it came, and up we went.

'Ugh!' cried the man, staring down in horror at the grisly spectacle. 'Oh, that's put my mind at rest!' Cheerfully he paid up – and he was to pay more.

About a fortnight later we were in the pub again, and heard that he was in trouble. Since the red-tailed rat had gone, there were more rats in his cellar than ever before. We knew how truly he spoke. So along I went, this time with Bill, and cleared him of rats as we well knew how, and were paid.

You might like to know a simple way of catching rats in a hedge bank, where they very often have large colonies; a simple way, but an effective one. You will want some old tins. Nestlé's milk tins we used to get, from the shoot on the Sewage Farm, and cut the bottom out to leave a clear run through. Tie an old stocking securely round each tin, and make sure there are no holes in the leg and foot, which are left hanging free.

We would take perhaps a score of these tins and stockings ready with us. Working softly so as not to bolt the inmates, we pushed the tins into the rat holes on the bank side, then stepped softly up on to the bank top. There we drove in the seeker, or searcher, a long iron rod with a ring handle at one end and a point at the other; the sort of thing any blacksmith can make. Down into the hard earth we pushed the rod, and shook it, and stamped with our feet; and out ran the rats into the tins, and so to the stockings, several together. A stick put paid to them.

Doughy the knife-grinder would be with us at times: a rough, tough, character, one who could hold his own in the roughest house; yet one who was always courteous to the opposite sex, and a man with a sense of humour, so that he was welcome everywhere.

One day when he was having a drink, the publican was bemoaning the loss of his dog. 'I must have another dog, a yard dog, and a good one,' he explained to the company. Some days later Doughy came in, and pushed something over the counter.

'Brought it for you!' he said. The man took one look.

'What do you call this, a dog? I said I wanted a yard dog.'

'Well; isn't that near enough?' Doughy asked innocently. 'Near enough three feet isn't he?' He had brought a Dachshund.

Another time, it was Christmas Eve, he was missing from his accustomed spot in his favourite pub, The Bricklayer's Arms at Edmonton. Before long in he walks with a bag, and two fine cockerel heads hanging over the side.

There was some astonishment, for everyone knew that Doughy could never afford to eat two chickens.

Somebody cried, 'Going to raffle them, Doughy?'

'I will if you like, boys, what about twopence a round, eh?' They fell for it, and it didn't take Doughy long to gather up a few shillings, with the bag standing proudly on the bar counter, and the cockerel heads looking alluringly down.

The draw was made, the lucky winner stepped up, took his prize – and stopped in consternation. He ripped open the bag. Out fell the two heads: the bottom was nothing but newspaper.

Silence in the bar. One or two guffaws. An oath from the winner and one or two cries to Doughy to hand back the cash.

Doughy only smiled. 'Be fair boys, be fair, you wanted me to raffle them, I never said they were cockerels, but if any gentleman hasn't had his money's worth, he can ask for his twopence back.' The laughs began, the winner of the heads joined in, and while they were calling him all sorts of names, Doughy wished them all a Merry Christmas and slipped out.

Even the butcher forgave Doughy. When he was hard up (and when was he not, with his unchanging rag of a suit, and his old scarf!) he would pause at the butcher's, look at a piece of meat displayed on the outside counter, pick it up and put it down again as we were allowed to do in those old unhygienic days, and then with a look of resignation, move on, dog at heel.

Before he could realise what was happening, out of the corner of his eye the butcher saw his meat disappearing off the counter and setting off down the road in the jaws of the cur that had just slunk by. For Doughy had said, 'Go back and get it!' and unerringly the dog had obeyed, for his master's word was law to him without question of rights and wrongs.

If that was wrong, as indeed it was, at least I have known others even more dishonest, and who did more harm with their ways.

What of the dog-stealers, who walked the streets with aniseed in the turn-ups of their trousers, or the parings or the frog from a horse's hoof, and enticed away little children's pets, so that they were never heard of again?

What of the two rascals who opened a boarding house for pets? A big empty shop, a ledger on the counter, and out at the back in the yard, a row of miserable boxes: the kennels for the pets?

People soon started coming, for as I have said, there is no fathoming the depths of gullibility, and the legend, 'Your Pets Boarded and Cared For' looked reassuring.

One man dressed in the only white coat they possessed, was always in attendance, for no one must be allowed to go through.

A client would come in, carrying her pampered over-fed lap-dog, full of concern for it and pity for herself, for she could not make the poor dear eat.

The white-coated one took the dog in his arms, opened its mouth, smelled its breath perhaps. 'Off his food, is he, madam? Leave him with us for a week – er – just a minute.'

He went to the rear of the shop, and opened the door. 'Charlie, any kennels vacant?'

'Numbers 27 and 35, sir!'

Back he would come, all smiles. 'Then that'll be all right. Just leave him with us. Our charge is a guinea for the week, madam.'

As soon as she was gone, the pet was pushed outside. 'Water only, Charlie, for three days.' And after, it was the bare minimum of food.

The end of the week brought the client, to find her pet overjoyed to see her and the man full of concern, stroking and fondling her darling. And if by some strange chance she had forgotten a titbit with which to tempt it, be sure the man had a piece of meat in his pocket, and the dog bolted it down whole, for hunger needed no second bidding.

Of course, the cure was the right one, for most of the troubles brought in were due to over-indulgence, and the men might have had a prosperous business. But after a while they began to persuade clients to leave their dogs a further term, for the cure to be completed; and to make certain of keeping them they would show how the hair had fallen out in places, and explain how the dog must wait till the hair was growing strongly again. And well they knew it would, for that distressing complaint had its origin in a pair of close-cutting scissors, or a few drops of diluted acid. Rogues they were, and their roguery extended far beyond the shop.

They hired a bookmaker's outfit, though they knew next to nothing of the game, went off to the races and set up beside the

OF DIVERS THINGS DONE

course. They wrote up the runners, and began shouting the odds. Luck was with them again, for a tipsy backer handed over a fiver to bet with. So excited were they to feel the thin crispness of it the 'bookie' forgot his receipt till his partner nudged him, whispering, 'Give him a receipt, give him a receipt!'

'Give him the whole lot!' said the bookie – and the two were having coffee and cakes safely away from the course, while their client was searching for his winnings. As I say, they were lucky, for they got clean away, but the law caught up with them in the end, over what was known as the Sovereign Trick.

Dressed for the part the two men would enter a pub, lean comfortably on the counter, and order two whiskies. As they were handed to them, one man would ring a sovereign down upon the counter and the two stood together to drink. The maid returned with the change, and placed it before them. With hand outstretched to take it up the man would pause, and say very gently, 'I'm sorry, ma'm, but I gave you a sovereign.'

'Yes, of course, but I gave you . . .'

The man regarded her with a stare, lifted his hand for her to see, looked down again himself: no half sovereign in the change. The maid, covered with confusion, hurried to make good the mistake: the two rascals drained their whisky, said their thanks, and were off – ten shillings the richer, for the first half-sovereign had been there right enough, till a deft flick of one finger had sent it into the open top of the second man's umbrella. But, as I say, they were caught in the act, and went to gaol, and the Home for Pets was closed.

I believed in keeping on the side of the law whenever possible, and my lapses at worst were only misdemeanours; if caught I went peaceably, as you will hear: even if in my heart I was remembering my father's adage – 'If ever you're fined, go again the next night when no one expects you, and take enough to pay for all you have lost.' And even Authority has its lapses.

I was going home one evening by train with a catch of goldfinches, when a policeman got into the compartment and sat opposite. He eyed me with a look that made me feel weak inside, for if ever a policeman knew a bird-catcher when he saw one, this was he.

'Been out?' he asked after a bit, by way of opening the conversation. I assented. 'Bird catching?'

'Been round the hedges and fields a bit.'

'Catch any?'

'I've got a few,' I agreed cautiously, not liking the way the talk was leading.

He leaned over confidentially. 'Any goldfinches?'

And the upshot of that little conversation was that I sold a goldfinch to a policeman – but I had to take it to his house myself, covered up and kept hidden. To be on the safe side I had the bird in a paper bag, so that if there were a trap, I could tear the bag, release the bird and be freed of incriminating evidence: for without the bird there could be no charge. But even the law I found can include bird-lovers, and bird-lovers were the people who kept us in trade.

Often they were tricked – not by the bird-catcher, but by the vendor – the man who used dabs of dye to make a hen bird appear a cock, for the sake of making a few pence extra. We knew our birds – from the nest. Any catcher worthy the name would tell in a glance whether a first plumage bird was cock or hen. Take the goldfinch for example; jet black on the shoulder, cock; black tinged with brown, hen. Goldfinches we could always sell, and when we sold a bird we knew we had a customer pleased and satisfied – one who would be glad to see our face again.

We used every means we knew to catch the birds they wanted.

I was not fond of lime for taking birds, but it was a ready way of getting goldfinches. All I needed was a stand of thistles or of teasels. Instead of the wire so many used for the limed perch, I used the wild grasses that Nature provided. In the heads of the teasels I bored a hole in readiness, then took the flowering stem of a grass, and drew it through the part-opened tin of lime to smear it from end to end, and broke the sticky thread with a quick snap at the end. Then I inserted the grass into the teasel head. I had not long to wait, for the birds love the seeds they find there. A goldfinch would come down, flutter and alight, with his legs on the sticky grass. But no goldfinch was ever caught as he alighted, for then his wings are closed. It is when he feels the lime on his feet and opens his wings to fly, that he is trapped, for then a wing is caught and held helpless. The bird may even see the lime stick lying there as he alights, but there is nothing he can do, for to escape he must open wings, and in a second he is fluttering on the ground, a prisoner. I would pick up my bird, rub off the lime with a little dust from the ground, or lick it off with my tongue.

When the birds were 'tricky', that is, birds that had learnt to fear man and his ways, I tried breaking off two of the stiff side bristles from the teasel head, liming them, and laying them crosswise on the head, a double snare for any bird alighting.

When I was working in thistles I used grass stems, or the bristles from a yard broom. The limed grasses I dropped loose among the thistle heads, but the bristles had more attention. To each I bound a pin, that I might stick them about the plants and make landing places for the birds. These bristles I kept in a lime tin; a container holding the glue, and with holes in the lid through which protruded the bristle ends, so that as each was drawn from the case, the lime was smoothed and trimmed off evenly along its length.

I have said we knew our birds: it proved useful in more ways than one. I was shooting near Cuffley, in a field close to the spot where the Zeppelin fell in the First World War, and I had been telling of the quantity of food a pigeon could hold. Half a pint of pure wheat I swore I could take from one crop, and was disbelieved. Without more ado, I took a pigeon from the bag, held it head down, and with the other hand pressed out from the crop all the wheat it had been stealing: and it just spilled over the rim of a half-pint glass. Pigeons are gluttons in their feeding, taking so much at a sitting they can hardly take to the air after. Twice a day they feed, at morning and evening.

If it is surprising how much a crop can hold, it is no less surprising what the contents sometimes are. I have known pigeons prepared for sale with crops heavy with sand and shot – for shot was cheap enough: and not only pigeons, chickens too were weighted to make them fetch a few shillings more.

And there was the long established custom of cobbing – of fattening ready for market. I had an aunt who regularly cobbed her fowls. Those destined for the butcher she fed forcibly, holding them upside down on her lap and pushing down their necks balls of mash, potato peelings, and old bread, then back on their perch they would go and underneath in the morning would be a fine heap of droppings. The birds put on weight as if by a miracle, and were worth shillings more when their end came.

There were many wrinkles we picked up, mixing with others in the same walk of life. If you had a chaffinch in a cage, and the bird would not sing, how could you make it sing? We tied a black handkerchief over the cage, hung the cage on a line out of doors where it could swing in the air, and that bird, perhaps because the movement simulated the sway of boughs would sing and sing in the dark, as blinded birds sang in their darkened days. I knew an old carter who had his bird slung under the cart, to the axle, and for mile upon mile that bird cheered his way.

Today of course it is a crime to take a singing bird from the wild to gladden the heart of young or old, though bird-lovers will flock to see a stranger that has made landing on our shores, and by their thoughtlessness destroy any chance it had of nesting. We may spray our crops to kill weeds and with them the insect life on which birds so largely depend, and even destroy at times the birds themselves.

There is much talk of the cruelty that went with bird catching in the old days, and there was cruelty, but there were people then who loved birds as there are today, and they cherished their pets. Bird-catchers included men who had birds that would come at a call – at a whisper – birds that acted as lure for their wild brethren with what in our pride we call human intelligence; and these birds were trained by kindness and patience: no man ever won the unquestioning confidence and trust of any creature by cruelty. Now the arts we used to bring our birds to us are forbidden and must one day be lost, but I can speak of them as one who has practised them all.

If you heard a chaffinch singing in a tree, and wanted him for the power and the beauty of that song, would you know how to catch him? We did: and though, when I have told you how, you may think it simple, as indeed in essence much of our work was simple, yet you must recall that years of endeavour and practice and patient learning went into the art of being a first-class bird-catcher.

In the month of February when the chaffinch was recalling his song and bringing it to perfection, I was much abroad in the woods, listening, appraising, remembering. Then in March, when, as we always said, the cock was singing to his hen, I would make my preparations.

Pegging a Chaffinch

I needed my singing bird in his covered cage, some limesticks, and a dummy chaffinch, carried in a tin in my pocket.

I came to the tree where the chaffinch was singing. Below the tree on the ground I placed my bird, with the dummy near. Now the bird in his tree hears a challenge, looks all about him, and sees nothing. He flies down, branch by branch, flies out and over my head: hears the singing from the ground, and spies the dummy. He comes and goes in anger and agitation; he flights to the ground and walks about the dummy bird, flirting wings, challenging. The bird makes no move; the chaffinch flies up into the air, and dives in to the attack, from the rear, always from the rear, to strike his rival at the back of the neck. He dives down and sweeps in – and there, just at the back of the bird, and right in the line of flight is my lime stick. He is entangled and caught, and I pick him from the ground. So fast do they come in at times I have known them fly right into the dummy and carry it with them for yards. This was the method known as pegging a chaffinch.

Sometimes it happened that a bird was too timid to make the attack – it sang and called and flew about, but would not come in to be caught. Then we had to resort to another method – simple, as I have said, yet calling for close observation.

Waylaying a Chaffinch

My singing bird was on the ground, the dummy might be on the ground or on the tree itself, for it was always set upon a twig with a nail projecting below the tail, and another below the middle of its body, that we might secure it where we wished.

Now, with birds singing on tree and ground, I step back to watch the one I want to take—the bird in the tree. I see his

sprightly step, his mincing way of walking that would tell me
'chaffinch' from a hundred yards away; I note the spots to
which he returns again and again in his flights about the tree,
for birds are creatures of habit: and I waylay him in those
very spots, sticking in my limed bristles where I know he must
come. And before long, down he flights, walks down a branch
a little way, flights down again, touches a bristle with a foot,
with a wing, and is mine. Pegging a chaffinch, and waylaying
a chaffinch, these were two of the arts we knew. And despite
all the laws, they are practised today, for there are people even
now who see no more wrong in taking a bird and caring for it,
than in taking wild mammals from their own land and keeping
them in a strange climate where they must soon die.

I make no pretence; catching for sale, and catching or killing
for food, were the forces that drove me.

There were park ducks that took their evening flight over
my very house as the light went from the earth to linger in the
sky. Where they went I had no idea at first, but I found out.
I went up to watch from the bedroom window: they were
dropping down, it seemed, into a cemetery. It did not take
long to find out why; they were going to an old moat, now
filled in. There were fish in the moat. While I waited I saw a
pike rise to the surface and snatch the matchbox I had thrown
away, as I have seen them take young greenfinches, too weak on
the wing to cross a pond, that have dropped near the surface.
But I was not after fish. I came again, with a gun. Some
time later the keeper in the park remarked that the ducks
seemed fewer than usual at this time of year. I forbore
comment.

At other times, and when conditions were right, I took ducks
with acorns. It was a cruel method, but then so are many
of the ways civilised peoples use to slaughter their food. There
was a family at home, waiting for me to return with the next
meal: I knew how to obtain it. I will tell you how. I hardened my heart, gathered a handful of acorns, made a split along
their length, inserted a fish hook into the slit with the barb
projecting, and a short length of line attached to the other end.
Then down I went to the shallows under the oaks where acorns
had fallen into the water's edge, and there I set my acorn

traps, and left them, while I went some hundred yards upstream, for ducks will not feed unless they see the bank free. Before long a duck would swim in, and then a fluttering and splashing of water told me I had made a catch: and I hurried over to put it out of its misery.

I have used the same bait for woodpigeons: laying the acorns in the grass, or under the November leaves when they had covered the fallen acorns.

You may condemn me for these things, even though I did them years ago, but recall the alternative. There was no real relief, and what relief was to be obtained had to be worked for. I had heard tell of men standing at a framework table, with a grid of iron before them and a lump of stone, and a hammer to break that stone into pieces small enough to go through the holes in the grid, when they fell through to the floor to be swept away. Breaking stones for roadmaking earned men the small pittance they were given: and many a long hour it might take to earn it. I preferred to feed my family by taking the gifts Nature offered all around: for the fields were my delight as they had been since boyhood.

I have told you of methods of taking rabbits: occasionally we used the gin trap too, that is now illegal.

In the spring when the buck rabbits were full of the urge to breed, I would catch a doe and skin it, scrape up the loose earth from the little latrines that rabbits scoop out for themselves, and rub the earth round inside the skin. Then I covered my gin trap with that earth, and knew I should catch a buck.

Out he would come, sniff, sniff, hopping big-eyed with desire – then sniff, sniff again at the scent of the doe, and stamp, stamp his little forepaws would go, and ping! he was prisoner.

The gin trap was cruel and so to my mind is the new humane trap, for a wild creature suffers not only the pain of a wound but the terror of being held. Many a trapped animal will inflict deliberately upon itself greater torture than the trap could cause, in order to be free.

The gin trap was cruel. Yet I have used it even to take the beautiful kingfishers, setting my gin on a stream-side post, and taking their feathers to make flies for fishing, as we took toll of all that might serve us.

Sometimes things came to us without the asking.

On the far side of a stream that bordered one of the lands I poached lay an ammunition factory, where all the girls coming out it was said, might be seen with pink and white complexions from the eating of sweet cordite. Be that as it may, I became friendly with a nightwatchman there, after he had allowed me to come on to his land to pick up my catch: and later I gave him a supper or two from my bag. He came to inquire what ammunition I used, and said that if I cared to keep silent about it and would have a look in a place he would show me, he might have a few cartridges for me.

I looked many times after that, till the piano was so heavy at home I couldn't shift it, for it had no insides but cartridges, and every one of his supplying. At least they came to a good end, for they helped to feed many people.

I once made the inside for another piano – at least, Sally and I did so, carving and smoothing each separate note. When we had finished every note played but one; and when that was put to rights we sold the piano and felt we had earned the money.

Some of the things we did for our family were wrong, some were strange, some today are reckoned as cruel, though at the time we did them they were generally accepted.

I take the cartridges that are so welcome, and refrain from thinking of their import. I stand and shoot a bird coming in swiftly, and the next moment reel from a blow in the eyes: the snipe has come in on the slant with the speed of a rocket, and for a week I am not fit to be seen, with two black eyes. I have to train greyhounds, as I shall tell later. I must stop them from turning to fight the next dog as they run, so I fit a collar armed with two spikes bent forward, and the dog is cured. Today I should be summoned for cruelty if I so much as put one on the neck of a dog.

But with all the things we did, we had our own standards of what was fair and right, and the man who could not conform to those, lived a solitary life.

I have told of the poacher who persuaded me to take the

cottage of rats, and of his desire that I should work with him. In the end I did for a while, sensing all the time that it must come to an end. It did.

We had been taking rabbits and I as the younger man had been carrying the bag, thirteen rabbits young and old.

We came to the sharing out. He bent over and sorted out two sixes, the larger ones for himself. 'What's this, you must have lost one,' he said, 'there's only twelve here!' I knew how many I had been carrying, and the weight of them, and I knew how many I had placed before him.

I took a punch at his back – 'Well, what's this, then!' I asked in anger, for there was the swelling of the lost rabbit. He was wearing one of the old cord waistcoats with a big sleeve pocket running round the body, and when I wasn't looking, he had pushed the rabbit in. I had said nothing to his unequal sharing of the rabbits, but this was the end. We might regard the rest of the world with some of the distrust with which it viewed our own deeds, but at least we had to have a trust in one another, as poaching families always have: and as we had been taught from earliest days to have, so that not one of us would ever have given another away. If ever we tricked another, it was in the spirit of devilment and fun.

Even Father could not resist. Once I brought home two birds I could not identify. Father looked at me as I showed him them. 'Boy,' he said, 'don't you touch those – poison they are!'

Going in next day, I found Mother with a bird, roasted delicately, on her plate, and another bird on Father's. 'Why,' I cried, 'I thought you said they were poison!'

'Ah! boy,' retorted Father, 'you'll learn, boy, you'll learn! They were water rails and many's the year since I had the chance of eating one', and he plunged in his fork.

9

The Bird-catcher

GUN, rod and snare gave me food to bring home to my family, good food, fare fit for any table in the land; and, in the days when their taking and selling were allowed, the birds of wood, field and hedge provided an income. I was a professional bird-catcher, with the cages, the call-birds and the nets of my calling, for only a professional could hope to compete with others. In everything, I had the finest I could buy, or make, or have made. When I married Sally, I wed, you remember, into a poaching family, and Sally's father made for me the finest bird-catching nets I ever possessed, eighteen yards long by five feet high; and yet so fine was the silk of which they were made, I could fold them up and put them into the poacher's pocket which Sally sewed into every jacket I had.

I walked the woods with call-birds and dummy to take chaffinches, pegging and waylaying as I have told. I went into the fields and laid nets to catch the bright goldfinches. I walked the hedges and hung my flue nets in the gaps, to take the birds as they passed along the hedge; greenfinch and linnet and bullfinch. The bullfinch I had to take with great tenderness from the pocket of the net, or it would die in my hand. At night I came to the hedge again, by stealth, carrying lantern and back-net.

I had to know not only how to catch birds, but how to keep them well and happy after, that they might fetch top price in the market. And I must know the songs that were in greatest demand, for in those days common working men knew the songs of their chosen birds as would few today. Bird fanciers held singing contests, and men followed the fortunes of a renowned bird as today they follow a footballer, a greyhound, or their favourite darts team.

As the darts team is welcomed at its pub and draws many into the bar, so the bird contests were in favour with publican and public alike. Nearly every bar had its singing bird, a good bird owned by the house, a challenge and a draw. The pubs themselves became noted for their contests, one as a goldfinch house, one a chaffinch, one a linnet. Close by the reservoirs I poached at Walthamstow was a goldfinch house, The Standard. Often, in these houses, you might see the cages of would-be champions, left by their owners to hang on the bar wall to accustom them to the smoke and confusion, birds looked after by the landlord and his staff.

On the contest night the bar filled early with supporters and aspirants each with his singing bird in its back cage covered with the traditional black handkerchief. Often it would be a chaffinch night, for the chaffinch was the best known of all the cage birds and the commonest, as it is the commonest bird in this country today.

As time draws near the drinks are finished and one and all make for the contest room, a quiet room, upstairs out of the noise and the bustle.

The first two contestants are called, the cages uncovered and hung with face to the wall.

Two judges are there, one for each bird.

'Stand back!'

Now the owners are with the crowd; they have done all they are permitted to do, the next ten minutes belong to the birds.

First one bird, then the other, completes a 'limb'; that is, a full song with a true ending, and for each limb the judges allot a point, the winning bird being the one that at the end of ten minutes has the greater number of limbs to its credit. His owner collects the prize money, for these duels of the birds were always for stakes.

The birds will sing no more tonight. There may be eight pairs of contestants in an evening, or the night may be the occasion of an individual match between two champions, with the whole house listening and appraising.

In the woods, I was listening always for contest singers.

The earliest bird to be taken was the chaffinch, for it begins to sing before the end of the flight season, the winter season of flocking and wandering. Then the birds were in mixed companies of cocks and hens, for all that people will tell you they stay separate in winter. They were mixed too in song, for they came from many different localities, and each district had its own characteristic song, so that a man who knew his birds might tell as soon as a bird had sung, whence it had come. In winter I might catch at Epsom, Cuffley or Chingford, and take birds from them all. But as the flight season ended, the birds returned to their own county and their own corner of it.

Then, when they sat in the trees fighting love's battle with song, seldom crossing into another's territory but obeying the message of the song, I could take the singers of my choice. Not every bird could be a good singer. I walked in the woods, listening, going softly, standing till I had placed the bird, the tree, the bough, and listening always for the rollic that would mark the bird a winner of contests.

'Old-Jack-White's-ear!' one would end, a good ending.

'Old-Joe's-broke-it!' another would say, and another sing the reply, 'Old-Joe-mend-it!'

I went down to Epsom and caught there, where the birds had another good ending, 'Chow-kiss-me-dear!'

I went into Middlesex, where I heard birds both bad and good. 'Jack-White's-here!' one would sing. 'Joe-Joe-Joe!' another would end, a bird I could not give away to a fancier, let alone sell.

I went into the woods at Cuffley, and a bird sang, 'Sweet-ear!' to end, another I liked to hear. And there at Cuffley, where I have pegged thirty chaffinches in a single day, I once caught a bird of magnificent voice, one of the finest singers I ever took: a three-in-the-mouth bird, ending with a treble 'Swett-hear-hear-hear!' and I had to waylay him after all, for he lacked the courage to fly down to attack the dummy or, perhaps, knowing the power of his own song, he relied on that to silence the other.

I took him to Club Row, the London bird-market, to sell,

confident that there I should find a buyer; and, knowing his value, I took brother Bill with me to hold the cage, for birds can be lost in Club Row, or could then.

It was not long before his voice was filling the air. Passers paused in amazement. Other vendors came with their birds, loud singers as they believed them, hoping to silence mine, as a strong singer may, but my chaffinch sang on unperturbed; 'Swett-hear-hear-hear!' he ended, singing with a fire and power they could not equal.

Toughs gathered round, demanding that I untie the handkerchief and let them see the bird. 'No!' I replied, confident in the power of my brother to hold off any number. 'No, he's costing you thirty shillings, unseen!'

They declared they would not pay it for an unseen bird. Off they went to The Crown, a pub renowned in the annals of bird lore, and there they asked the loan of the landlord's own bird, to see if it might silence mine. It failed. Back they went, to fetch the landlord himself to hear the bird.

'Can I see it?' he asked.

'No!' For I knew that brought out into the light of day, he might cease to sing. 'But it's a good bird, not a feather out of place.' That was to reassure him, for now and again a baldheaded bird was palmed off unseen, a bird that would never grow feathers in a cage.

'You're a regular here, aren't you?'

'Yes,' I answered, 'and I never sell a dud bird, not to the likes of you people anyway.'

'I'll take a chance on it. Here's your thirty shillings.'

'Now you can untie him. There he is, never moulted in a cage, a fresh bird, and a champion!'

Within a few weeks he had proved me right, for he had won contest after contest, and earned the nickname of Robert the Devil, the singer no bird could stop.

He was loaned to gang after gang, travelling from one house of contest to the next by cab, winning profit wherever he went.

At last Robert the Devil had sung his last song, but his travels were not ended. He was stuffed and mounted in a show case, and made the rounds still as the bird that none had silenced. You may wonder that I did not keep such a bird for myself, but my joy was not in the smoke of bars, but in the open air and the singing woods.

I took another chaffinch, no good for contest, but a splendid draw to bring others down to my limed dummy. 'In a week or two's time we'll see a wheatear!' they sang overhead in their trees. 'Lob-Lob-Lob-chuck-weed-ur' my bird would end from the ground, and so slowly that men who knew him would exclaim, 'Ah, there he goes again, up to Liverpool Street and back!' a good train journey for us; so slowly he sang, a bird might hit the limed dummy before he had completed a song.

But of all the chaffinches, the most prized was a Chingford bird, from Epping Forest in Essex. No man ever sold a bird as coming from Chingford unless it had, for when that bird came into song again, which would be about three weeks from the date of its capture, the fraud would be immediately known, and it would go hard with that man if he were seen again in Club Row. Many and many a Chingford bird I had, walking through the Forest and on through the woods as far as Ongar, listening always for the ending, 'Chuhweedur!' or 'Chuckwaydur!', ending always in an 'r'.

'Bell-bell-bell-la-la-la Chuhweedur!' they sang.

'Bell-bell-bell-la-la-la-Chuckwaydur!' ringing in the woods I loved, and as I loved to hear them, though I took the cage to be their prison.

The chaffinch was the commonest bird in a cage, but no bird was better loved than the little goldfinch.

I have caught and sold thousands upon thousands of them, catching at times as many as four or five hundred in a week: yet always I felt the goldfinch was one of God's birds, born a lover of the open lands and the free air. And still I caught, as others did, to earn a living.

I capture nine in one pull of the nets, and I say to myself as I take the quick flutter of their bodies into my hand, 'Three there are to live, three to linger, and three to die.'

I do all I know to save them. I take them home, and give them the half-freedom of the aviaries at the back of the cottage. I bring to them the wild seeds they have loved, thistle and teasel, and knapweed, the waste seeds gathered from the harvest fields and the hedgerows.

Three feed, and they will live. Three more will feed, but only on the black niger seed, a foreign seed they have never found in the wild: and they can only linger and then die, for in a few weeks the seed will have burnt out their stomachs. These I must sell quickly, for only occasionally can I get them to eat their own life-giving seeds. I try. I take a tame bird, one long used to the cage, and place it among them and cover them all with an old curtain; and there, in the quiet darkness and with time, seeing their brother feed, some of the wild ones come to their feeding. But never those that, having lost their freedom, are determined to die. Yet I try for them too. I crouch by their cage, where they sit, head under wing. All day I sit, and all night after, willing them to live, waking them every few minutes to show them their water and their seed, the wild seeds that will save them, the black niger that may tempt them back to feeding. They take none; they put head back under wing; they will die, for their hearts are broken.

But when I sold a singing goldfinch, what hearts were gladdened to hear him, for in those days there were still many homes that knew nothing of the country, of its fields and flowers; and nothing of its birds beyond the little singer that hung on its nail in the sun.

'Widdle-widdle-su-whitty!' one bird would sing, a fine contest bird, such as I might hear at The Standard in Walthamstow.

'Sippitt-sippitt-ker!' another would sing. And, as a Chingford chaffinch was famed above all others, so there was a goldfinch all bird-catchers sought.

'Slam-slam-su-whitty!' the bird began, so that it became known as a slamming goldfinch. Today if such a bird could be found and caged, it would bring its owner a small fortune, but it is years since I heard, or heard of, one, and that song I must believe is extinct. The last birds I ever heard to sing it belonged to a barber in Edmonton, and bird and barber are both long gone. In the old days, when a man had such a bird, he would use it as a schoolmaster, keeping it in a room with perhaps a dozen young birds, that some might learn the song and sing it for their own; for birds learn much from one another, as the chaffinch in the flight season mimics another's song, and keeps it for his own.

The linnet was another singer often caged, a favourite both for contest and for a pet in the home.

'Tollic-tollic-icky-qay-bargee-weet!' one would sing, and another make answer, 'Tollic-tollic-icky-qay-gypsy-weet!'

I cannot tell the numbers of linnets that I took, for they are among the easiest of birds to catch. I used bird-lime, I caught them in clap-nets, I lured them into trapping cages, I took them again by night from hedge and thicket.

At night I had a companion, one to walk the far side of the hedge, carrying a stick for beating. I chose the side with the moon behind me, or if there were no moon, I carried a lantern. To catch the birds I used back-nets, such as we used for the taking of sparrows in the ivy. When I came to a likely place, I shone the light, and held it aloft with the back-net: the stick smashed into the hedge on the far side, and out came the birds, greenfinch and linnet, not scattering but flying direct for the light and into my net.

Of all the birds that sang in a cage, the most imitative was the plump and lovely bullfinch, so sturdy looking but so highly strung; and that yet, taken young, could be taught to repeat almost any tune whistled to it. I knew one that sang perfectly both 'Pop goes the Weasel!' and 'God save the King!' as it was then.

Many a tale I could tell of the birds, for their ways and their capture filled much of my days, but perhaps I should tell a few of the tricks that were played upon the ignorant.

I think of the goldfinch, cock and hen so alike, a handful of gold and black and crimson feathers; so alike that few beyond the experts could know from the crimson which was which. I have sold thousands of them, always the hens first, and always as cocks. I have had people pushing and struggling to get to the birds to buy one before they were all gone, and over their heads a policeman at the back calling in stentorian tones that he wanted 'that bird', and that a hen like all the rest.

If you wish to buy a goldfinch, go to a reputable dealer, one who will give you a guarantee, or wait till you have heard the bird sing before you buy.

THE BIRD-CATCHER

As with goldfinches, so there was cheating over linnets.

'There you are, ma'm!' a dealer calls. 'There you are, seven white flights he's got. Here you are, see for yourself,' and he spreads the little wing over his fingers. 'Count 'em, m'dear, seven white flights he's got!' And seven it had, but the cock's white margin touches the centre of the feather, and this was a hen.

Other men sold hens as cocks, showing the crimson breast they had coloured with red ochre.

Even the greenfinch from the hedge, worth no more than fourpence, was made to bring in half a crown or three shillings, for it was colour-fed for some six weeks with red pepper, and changed into a canary; one that hung up in its cage would stay yellow about as long as it had taken to make it so.

Then there were the dyed birds; 'painted', people say, but they were dyed. Many a common bird has changed hands at a good price as a novelty after being dipped into a warm solution of permanganate of potash to turn it mauve, then dried in sawdust.

You may smile at the gullibility of people then, but they are swindled today. I still see colour-fed birds displayed for sale, and budgerigars sold as young that are so old they must be grandfathers several times over.

And of course the bird protection societies are caught too. Despite all the facilities that exist today for getting into the countryside, despite all the books and films that show the birds as they live, there are still people willing to pay to have a singing bird of their own; and catching goes on today in defiance of all the laws: in the season hundreds of birds are taken every week into captivity.

They have rings when you buy them, of course, rings that have been split and sealed again so that no join shows, and none may know that but a brief week or so ago those birds flew free in the sunshine. Or the rings are put on and the nestlings left till old enough to take.

In some ways times are easier for the catcher today. Competition is less, apparatus is easy to come by if you know where to seek, new methods come in with new materials. The goldfinch is taken with the nets ladies use for their hair; plentiful and cheap, and so light a dozen or more may be put into an envelope and concealed about the person.

The would-be catcher walks about the fields, unnoticed. He looks for a bed of teasel or of thistle that still holds a full harvest of seed. He waits, watching to see where the birds come and at what time, for tomorrow they will be here again, in this very spot at the same hour, passing on their rounds of the fields. But tomorrow the plants where they feed now so happily will be laced with hair-nets. A bird alights. His feet go through the net. He struggles to fly up, is enmeshed and falls helpless; as the rabbit, with head in the long net, struggles to push through, only to put legs into another hole. And when the birds are safely hidden, the hair nets are taken away, to leave no trace, and there is no lime to wipe from the bird.

I neither condemn nor do I condone. They do as I would have done years ago; but now they run the gamut of laws that were not in existence then, laws meant to be enforced, with vigilant men to see that they are.

Do not think that we looked upon ourselves as cruel men, any more than the butcher or the poulterer is today. We caught for a market: the art of the catcher was to take alive and to keep alive. Nor did we consider cruel a man who took home his bird, and hung it in its darkened cage on a line, where it might sing to the sunshine it had lost. With the air moving the cage till it seemed like a moving bough, the bird became used to the swinging of its prison, and when it was carried to contests had no fear.

But there were, largely among the most ignorant, people who would not be bothered to cover a bird to train it, but put out its sight so that it lived for ever in the dark. Those who cared nothing for the opinions of others, blinded the eye with a needle, piercing the pupil, and that eye turned white and might be told at once. Others, no less cruel but not wishing to see the blinded eyes, nor to have them seen, used a hypodermic needle and Indian ink, destroying first one eye, and then, some weeks later, the other, with the bird meanwhile turning its head constantly to one side, in order to use the eye that was left. As they blinded birds to make them sing, so ignorant people split their tongues to better that song, though that it could never do.

THE BIRD-CATCHER

Unavoidable cruelty in the taking of birds, and the cruelty of ignorance later, were blots upon our calling. Yet many cherished their birds and loved them deeply. I have known rough men, brutal men, who thought more of their singing bird than they did of wife and child. I have seen their bird cages, made from the finest mahogany, french polished, with perches made of ivory, and with silver drinkers of beautiful design. There was nothing too good for their birds, and, provided they were not blinded but sang in the gloaming of a handkerchief, then I say they were happy birds, for only from contentment and a full crop does a bird sing its best.

There was so much we had to know, some of it only to be gained by years of watching in the fields, some common sense. We never caught for instance, after a long period of rain, when all the thistle heads stood draggled and limp with the seeds soft within them, for the birds, taken home and given dry seeds would assuredly have died.

I have taken so many birds, holding their fluttering hearts against my hand; and known many of their life stories after: some happy, so that I could laugh as I think of them and others that bring the tears close. There was cruelty, but at least I brought joy into many a home.

My own brother had two redpolls which I had given to him, and which he loved and cared for himself, teaching them to draw up a little chain to reach their food and water, and letting them fly free about the room with window wide open, as budgerigars will today.

When he was but five years old he fell ill with pneumonia, in the days before an easy cure was known, and grew steadily worse.

One of his last requests as he lay dying was that we should let his birds out that they might sit on the iron rail of his bed as was their habit.

So it was done, while Father took him in his arms, and blew breath into him, to try to save him.

As he saw that all was vain, and laid the little body down, the birds left the rail, and flew out of the window and away from that house, never to return.

I Meet with the Law

A BIRD-CATCHER is not entirely free to choose where he will catch; to be successful he must go where the best singers are. So it was that in later years when the catching of birds was meeting with opposition, I found myself at times in an area where the taking of birds was prohibited, where it was my wits against those of Keeper and R.S.P.C.A.

One April morning I was in the forbidden area of Epping Forest. Behind me a nightingale chug-chug-chugged in the thicket, then poured out the beauty of his song, for the Forest had many a haunt of these birds. He threw back and forth across the glades song that no lover of birds could listen to unmoved. But though I heard him throbbing and keening and filling the air with passionate notes, my ear was for another song overhead in an oak, the song of a chaffinch, a Chingford chaffinch. Another, my call-bird, was on the ground below in his cage with the limed dummy near by, for I meant to take the singer in the tree.

And then, as I waited quietly, half-hidden against my thicket, I saw a figure dressed in brown, gun under arm, retriever at heel, come into the open glade: a Keeper, with the badge of his office against his brown coat.

He had not noticed me, but came on at peace with the world. Then, almost at his feet, a bird sang, slow and majestic, to end with a 'Lob-lob-lob-Chuckweedur!' It was my call-bird from his cage.

The Keeper glanced down, saw cage and dummy, looked

around, and saw me half in the thicket, and my bicycle leaning against an oak near by. There was no escape. My bird that had been so stout a friend, that had lured so many to the lime-stick, had given me away. 'Lob-lob-lob-Chuckweedur!' I heard him end again.

'Come on out,' cried the Keeper, 'come on, I've got you for bird catching.'

He picked up the dummy with its limed stick, and the cage with its handkerchief, and made towards my bicycle.

'What are you going to do with those?'

'I'm going to have you summoned for bird catching in Epping Forest.'

'All right,' I said, 'you treat me fair, and I'm your man,' an answer I had always ready, and one that often disarmed suspicion.

He took command of my bike and started off in the direction of Chingford. We came to the Plain, with me walking beside him, turning things over.

We passed the site of the Easter Fair that is held there on the Plain. 'You don't think of taking me through town like this, do you?' I asked. I had little stomach for being marched through the main street of Chingford with all eyes upon me.

'Just that,' he said. 'You try to run, and I'll shoot.'

I knew that was mere bluff: he wouldn't have shot in any case, and with the cage and the bicycle, he couldn't.

I decided to run for it. I walked quietly with him some yards more, then suddenly cut off into the Forest on my right, running for all I knew.

So I came home, by way of Plum Pudding Hill (or Yardley Hill as most have it) and there, seeing the possibility of lean times ahead, I went straight to the Labour Exchange to sign on. Inside, was brother George, drawing money for Father.

'I've been caught bird catching this morning,' I whispered, 'and the Keeper's taken my bird and the bike. Come with me this afternoon, and we'll get them back.'

It was a long walk from home, but our legs were used to miles, and in the Forest so long as there was the sun by day or the stars shone at night, we should never be at a loss for the way.

Darkness was coming as we reached the Keeper's cottage. I knocked at the front door. 'Who's there?'

'Curtis. You took my bike this morning, and I've come for it.'

The door opened a little, and a pair of eyes looked us over suspiciously. 'You'll get nothing, clear out of it,' the Keeper snapped, and shut the door.

'Come on,' whispered my brother, 'we'll give him a fright.'

We walked noisily down to the gate, waited a moment or so, then crept back up the path. I gave George time to get round to the back of the house, then I banged on the door; there came more bangs at the back. I rapped hard on the window; my brother banged and rapped at the back.

Then we fell silent, and after a moment's quiet, I stole back to the window. The Keeper was loading up his gun. He laid it carefully on the table and went from the room.

'Come on, quick,' I cried, 'he's gone to the 'phone.' And in my imagination I swore I heard the ringing of the bell as we made off down the little path. 'Let's get along the road a bit,' I urged, 'he's fetching the police.' We set off at a run.

Sure enough, we were barely a quarter-mile from the cottage when we saw three lights coming towards us – three policemen on bicycles.

We slowed to a walk, and watched the three go by.

As soon as they were well past, I hailed them: 'You off to the Keeper's?' My brother looked scared. 'Leave this to me,' I whispered.

The three bicycles had slowed down and stopped. One of the men called back, 'Why, is there trouble?'

'Yes, he's surrounded by a gang, we're the gang.'

The three lamps wheeled round and came back.

'The Keeper caught me bird catching this morning, and took my bicycle. We came up for it this evening, but I saw the Keeper had a double-barrelled gun on the table, so we ran for it.'

'Right, you come along back with me.'

So back we went, and knocked again at the garden door.

'Clear out, or I'll shoot,' came the voice from within.

'Open the door,' the Sergeant cried, 'this is the police.'

I MEET WITH THE LAW

The door was opened.

The Keeper caught sight of me. 'They're the ones. They threatened to shoot me. They've never left the place this last half-hour, the whole gang of them,' he poured out.

'That may be,' said the Sergeant, 'but we met these two men about a quarter of a mile down the road. They told us there was trouble here.'

'Trouble! They're bird-catchers: they came here looking for trouble, and they're armed.'

I put my hands over my head. 'Search me, and see if I've got anything!' I said. A policeman ran his hands over me, then over my brother.

'Nothing here,' said the Sergeant. 'Do you want to charge these men?'

'Yes, with threatening; and bird catching – both of them.'

'Then you'll have to come down to the Station.'

'Not tonight. I'm not going through the woods at night with those men.'

The Sergeant took out his notebook, and turned to us: 'Name and address?'

We gave them. 'I'm living at Edmonton now,' I said, 'but I was born at Waltham Abbey, and lived there for years.'

'Waltham Abbey, you say. D'you know anybody there now?'

'Yes, my Uncle Tucker.'

'What, Tucker Archer?'

'That's the one.'

The Sergeant turned. 'All right, Keeper, let Curtis have his bike. I'll be responsible for him, I know the family.'

So we came home, with the bike but without my birds, and in due course trouble followed on their account as it was bound to do, in the shape of a summons to appear at Stratford.

A summons for my brother as well, though he had been at Edmonton while I was bird catching. Worse still, I was charged with having threatened to shoot the Keeper.

Father went to Stratford with us, partly because he knew the Keeper and had no particular friendship for him, partly to help if he could.

The threat to shoot was taken first, and soon disposed of.

The Sergeant gave evidence of having found us a quarter-mile from the cottage and told how we had been searched without sign of a weapon.

Then came the bird-catching charge. I pleaded 'Guilty', my brother 'Not Guilty'. He swore he had been at the Relieving Officer's, and produced written evidence to prove it; and the charge was dismissed.

The Magistrate at last summed up my case.

'You have pleaded Guilty to bird catching. You come here to our Forest, taking our birds, and when the Keeper apprehends you, you threaten to shoot him.'

'Begging your pardon, your worship,' I cried, losing my temper, all I had at the moment to lose, 'but the shooting charge has already been dismissed, and they're not your birds any more than mine, and I'm still allowed to catch birds elsewhere.'

A titter in court. A call for silence. I knew that I should be fined now.

Three heads bent together in consultation.

Then came the sentence: One pound and fourteen shillings fine, my gear to be confiscated and the bird to be destroyed.

I left the dock and was led to a back room. My brother was there, and Father waiting to pay my fine. Coming out, whom should we meet but the Keeper.

'Good day, Ananias,' said my father bitterly, and passed without another word.

And so I went back to bird catching, remembering Father's axiom, 'If you're fined, go back at once to the same spot, and take enough to repay all you've lost.'

Some three weeks later, I was back in Club Row, selling birds as usual. After the sale, we went as our custom was, to a coffee shop to have a warming drink.

As we sat with our steaming mugs, there above our heads out of reach was a row of bird cages, each with its occupant and its black handkerchief, a whole shelf of cages each touching the other. These were the birds left by fanciers, some for sale, some to learn the songs of other birds. Song after song throbbed through the warm room.

Then my heart gave a leap. Somewhere along the row a

bird had begun a song, slow and powerful. I waited for the ending: 'Lob-lob-lob-Chuckweedur!' I turned to my brother, 'It sounds like my old bird!'

'It is. Which cage is it?'

'I'm going to ask at the counter.'

'Which, that slow chaffinch over there? He's a good bird, cost you a pound.'

'Can I see it please?'

He lifted it down, and took off the handkerchief. And there it was – my own bird, with its cage and drinker. Nothing had been destroyed. I paid the pound.

'Come on, George,' I said, 'I'm going to see that Keeper again.'

This time I went alone.

He was digging in the garden as I walked up to the cottage with the bird-cage carefully hidden.

He heard me coming, and looked up. He recognised me at once. 'Get out of my place!' he shouted.

'You might be getting out yourself, before I'm done.'

'What do you want?'

'Nothing. I've got all I want.'

'What do you mean?'

I unwrapped the cage and held it up. 'Ever seen this bird before?'

The Keeper pushed his fork into the earth, and stared at the cage as he might at a ghost.

'Some people would be interested to know what you do with property you are told to destroy.' I was watching his face, feeling almost sorry for him, though I didn't show it.

'Never mind,' I said, 'I've got the name and address of the man you sold these to.' (Which was half-true.) 'Well, you told me to go, I'm off.'

'Wait a minute!' This was a different man talking now, in a different voice. 'Come inside, we may be able to come to a solution.'

Come to one we did: I was never caught bird catching again in Epping Forest.

I am Caught Again

AT the time I tell of now, the screw had begun to turn. It was to end in a stranglehold that put the bird-catcher outside the law. But as yet no one was sure of himself. Rules that were to become law had not yet been decided, and if they had they were not universally applied. It was difficult both for the bird-catchers themselves, and for the Officers of the Royal Society for the Prevention of Cruelty to Animals who tried to put an end to catching. When it came to a court case, a man accused of taking birds might, by keeping his wits about him, defeat the Society officers, the Hughies as we always knew them.

If there should seem to you a strain of conceit in the tales as I tell them, you must remember that every time we secured a victory we saved for a little longer not only our own livelihood, but that of all brother bird-catchers. We had cause to try to win by our wits, cause for congratulation when we succeeded. Above all we had no time for the Societies, nor for the Hughies, however right their cause. They were taking away our living.

They would come, two of them together, to Club Row on a Sunday when bird selling was at its height, and pounce on one or two of us for overcrowding birds in store cages. They did not arrest us, a policeman was required for that; they took our name and address, and in due course just as we were congratulating ourselves that all had blown over this time, the summons would come.

I AM CAUGHT AGAIN

Three times in a few weeks I appeared at court upon a charge of overcrowding, and three times I was able to ask the same question, 'What size cage must I use to keep a bird in?' And since the Hughie did not know, and since there was no rule to tell him, and since I could buy a similar cage anywhere in England (and they are still offered for sale in Club Row in this year of 1960), three times I was let off.

A fourth summons came. This time I had no chance to ask a question, my face was known. It was ten shillings costs.

I was escorted from the dock to pay my fine. 'Got you this week, Curtis,' said the Sergeant with a cheery smile. 'Ten shillings, please!'

'I haven't got ten shillings, I haven't even ten ha'pennies on me.'

'All right, you sit and wait for the Black Maria!' as the Police Van was known in those days.

I sat down, quite prepared to wait a while.

Each time he arrived with a new client to pay a fine, the Sergeant said, 'You going to pay that fine, Curtis?' Each time the answer was, 'I can't!'

At long last came the occasion I was waiting for. 'Court closed!' he announced as he came in, and started gathering up the books. 'Now what about you, Curtis, and that ten shillings?'

'It's no good, I can't pay, and you won't be able to keep me after six o'clock,' I reminded him, 'not without a meal. And by the way, I wasn't given a period to pay in, was I, only a fine of ten shillings?'

The Sergeant stared hard at me, turned to a constable standing by, and nodded to him: 'Open that door, constable. Now, Curtis, get!'

And out I got, quickly, fearing to feel a boot behind me, and down the three steps I came from Old Street Police Station to freedom, and home.

A few days later came a knock at the door: it was a man from the Society come, he declared, 'for the ten shillings costs'.

'I'm very sorry you've been troubled,' I said, for I was never one to make bother without need, 'but I've no money till

I catch a few more birds, then perhaps you may get it, but it'll be in ha'pennies, as my wife buys the milk.'

He looked daggers at me as I closed the door, softly, irrevocably.

That made the fourth Hughie I had met on four different charges, and I was to meet them all again, together. Whether they talked among the bird-dealers and discovered where I had been in the habit of catching my birds I do not know, but at last they caught me red-handed, as they thought.

On a morning in early spring I had got up before dawn, and gone over with all my catching gear to my old ground, McMullen's farm at Cuffley. There I had laid nets for chaffinches with call-birds and brace-birds, and had already taken a single chaffinch. I was to be glad later that I had caught no more.

It was chill work, and my hands were stiff with it. I got down under the hedge out of the morning breath, and made a little fire of twigs. I was just toasting myself a piece of bread when there was a crashing in the hedge behind, and two men burst through, one a policeman, the other obviously a Hughie, with knickers and gaiters.

'Got you! You're bird catching!' the Hughie cried.

'Yes, and I'm allowed to catch in Hertfordshire, and on this farm, by permission.'

That stumped him for a moment, but I could see him staring out at my nets. I caught the eye of the policeman; I knew him; I had shot a couple of rabbits for him a short while before. He shook his head, to tell me that it was no wish of his to be there.

Meantime the Hughie was walking towards the nets; we followed. 'He's got brace-birds!' he exclaimed, and then, to me, 'Here, take up those birds, and the nets!'

'No,' I said, 'I'm touching nothing. If you want them, you take them up, and mind you don't break anything.'

Well, they tried, but they had no idea how to begin, let alone finish the job; the taking up of a pair of sixteen yard nets is a skilled job, and takes learning.

They made another appeal to me.

'All right,' I said, 'you start carrying the call-birds' (I had nine of them in cages there at the time), 'and put them down under the hedge, and I'll get things ready.'

I did. No sooner were they well away than I picked up a brace-bird, slipped off the brace, threw it away, and let the bird go free.

I did the same with the second, but as I threw the bird into the air, the Hughie turned and saw me, and back they both came at a run.

'Look at that!' the Hughie cried in disgust. 'He's done away with the evidence!'

He towered above me so threateningly I thought he was going to knock me down, but I could afford to go easy, knowing that he had no brace-bird left, and no evidence against me.

Then I remembered something – the chaffinch I had caught. It was with another brace-bird, but without a brace, in a small store cage.

'I'll take this,' I said, and picking up the store cage set off towards the hedge as if to put it with the others. Then, with some yards' start, I swerved and tore off into the field, ripping off the lid of the cage as I ran, trying to shake the birds out. One, I saw take to the air and find freedom; then the men were upon me.

'He's cheated us again!' the Hughie cried. 'Wait a minute though, what's this? Here's a chaffinch with a broken leg!'

And so it was. A thing that no bird-catcher would ever willingly do, damage his catch, I had done; and at the very worst of times. The chaffinch must have caught a leg in the wire of the cage, and trying to shake the bird free, I had broken its leg.

'Come on,' the man cried, almost beside himself with delight. 'We've got you now, we're taking you in!'

There was no sense in resisting. I helped them with the nets, packed up the gear professionally, and carried it to the road: and there I put it down.

'Well, if you want me at the Police Station, you'll carry it!' I said; and pretty heavy I knew it was, with everything packed ready.

They argued; they threatened; it was a long walk to the Station, and the sun was beginning to grow warm, but in the end they carried it, turn and turn about. A very hot job they found it, not being used to that load, as we were.

Before they were half-way to the Station, the policeman attempted to persuade the Hughie to let me go and summon me in the usual way, but he would have none of it, feeling victory within his grasp.

And so at last they reached the Station and were relieved of their burden: and I was informed that I should need to be bailed out.

I settled down to a long wait. A constable came at length to tell me that my address had been verified, and that my brother was coming to bail me out. I saw the time creeping round to six o'clock again, and then, there was my brother armed with my rent book, to prove that I was a bona-fide householder.

As I was leaving, I turned to the policeman in charge and said, 'If you're not giving me back my gear, take great care of it, it's expensive, and if anything happens to it, I shall be claiming for it.'

Before many days the summons came. I was to appear at Hatfield Police Court, on two counts, one of cruelty to a chaffinch, the other of confining birds in catching cages; that is, the small cages in which I kept my call-birds.

Before I was due to appear, I went up to Club Row, and from a big dealer's I brought two brand new whitewood catching cages, similar to those I had been using.

The day came. I looked round for my Hughie, and there I saw not only him, but all the others who had been on my cases. I saw their heads go together, with a nod or two in my direction.

'It looks bad,' I thought, 'they're obviously out to make it hot for me.'

My case came on. The policeman gave his evidence. 'Has the accused any questions to ask the witness?'

'No, your worship.'

I turned to the Hughies, waiting to see my last acquaintance come up.

Then an inspiration came to me. I turned to the magistrate: 'Begging your pardon, your worship, but would you allow the witnesses to stand outside till called for?'

I AM CAUGHT AGAIN

This was granted, and out they filed into the corridor; and a cold morning it was outside the court especially in those corridors.

Then the Society Officer who had caught me was called upon to give his evidence. He made everything as bad as possible for me, telling how I had been caught destroying the evidence and of how I had offered to fight them both, and had called them all the blackguard names under the sun, with words too bad to repeat, and ended by telling how I had tried to throw away my birds, and had done so, with the exception of one chaffinch that had been unable to get away, and they had discovered it had a broken leg.

When he had finished he had told such a mixture of truth and untruths, I hardly knew how to begin to unravel them, though the bird's leg I could have explained.

I looked at the honest country faces before me, and decided to leave everything to them.

'Any questions to ask the witness?'

'No, your worship, but if you will grant me the return of the previous witness to verify some of this man's statements I will be greatly obliged.'

The policeman came back into the witness-box. My first was a simple question. 'Did I want to fight you when I was caught?'

Now I am about five feet ten, and they were both six footers, and unlike me they were heavy with it: and I had had no breakfast.

The policeman smiled down, as much as to say, I'd have liked to see him try. 'No, your worship, he came quietly enough.'

I thought I saw a gleam of sympathy, of friendship, before me. 'Any more questions to ask the witness?'

'No, your worship.'

There came the overcrowding charge. I produced the cages I had bought in Club Row. 'These,' I said, 'are what I was using, and here is the receipt from the cage-makers.'

That was all, and that finished the case as far as I was concerned.

The court rose, and went into a little side room while I waited in the dock. They were gone for a few minutes only.

Now came the sentence.

'Alfred Thomas Curtis, you have been found guilty of cruelty to a chaffinch, but there have been in our opinion so many lies told in this case [they used the word, 'lies'] that we have decided to give you the benefit of the doubt. The overcrowding charge is dismissed. You will be fined four shillings for cruelty and for catching birds, and your nets and birds are to be confiscated.'

My Hughie jumped up in a rage, and made towards the witness-box. 'Begging your pardon, your worship, but there are vet's fees of fifteen and six.'

'The prisoner's case is closed. You will have to take the money from the Poor Box. Case closed.'

I went from the dock into a side room. There I said to the constable, 'You can't confiscate my gear, I'm not here for bird catching, and in any case I'm allowed to catch birds in Hertfordshire, and Cuffley's in Herts.'

'Come to think of it, you're right. Wait here while I see the usher.'

Before long he was back. 'All your gear is to be returned.'

But when I came to collect it, I found a strange state of affairs. It had already been shared out among the Station staff. Most had something at home: many, it turned out, were bird fanciers themselves. Two of my call-birds were dead, but for those, and any missing gear, I was paid cash, and came home at last with more in my pocket than I had taken with me.

Nobody was more surprised to see me coming home with my gear on my shoulders, and a smile on my face, than the neighbours. Now I was able to go round to the pawnbroker's and reclaim Sally's wedding ring, which I had pawned for a pound to help pay the fine I had expected. It may seem strange to you that I should pawn it, but the pawnbroker was to us the moneylender, and some articles might go many times to his shop without ever changing hands.

I have appeared in court a number of times, but always for misdemeanours, not for crimes. A five pound note, I suppose, would cover all the fines I have paid, but a different tale it would have been had I been fined for the things that were never discovered.

Of Greyhounds and Toys

THE greyhound racing of today is a vast and well-organised business, but I recall some of its early beginnings, and indeed had a part in some of them.

Two brothers, one a bookmaker, one with a breaker's yard, gave me my introduction to the racing of those days. Whether they knew that I had no regular employment at the time, or knew that I had been poaching all my life and understood animals and their needs, or whether it was just that I knew how to use the pair of hands I was given I cannot say, but one of them asked if I would build some kennels for greyhounds. I undertook to make eight to begin with, and set to work. After a week or more of loneliness I began to wonder when my employer was going to put in an appearance, and pay me for work done.

Then one day there came into the yard a man, stamping around flatfooted and fuming with anger.

'My lazy, indolent, incompetent chauffeur brings me to this,' he exclaimed. 'I've had a wonderful ride, in a lorry! Who are you?'

'I'm the man who makes the kennels here.'

'Where are they?' I showed him.

'How much do they come to?'

'There are eight, at two pounds a time.'

He went over to examine them, and very fine they looked, with the tops of the doorways grilled with brass rods – old stair rods from his brother's yard, polished till they winked at him.

'Might as well pay you now,' he said, and promptly did.

'Ah,' I thought, 'an angry man, but an honest one and a ready payer,' so that I was pleased to be working for him. This was the bookmaker, 'Shallow', with whom I was to have many dealings.

It was not long before he asked whether I would like the job of looking after his greyhounds and training them. 'I've never trained dogs for racing,' I explained. 'My dogs have had to work for me in the field.'

'I want a man who knows animals,' he said, 'you've been with them all your life.' At that, I took on the job.

I was not allowed it all my own way at first. His brother I found was against me in many things. He refused to let the dogs have water to drink, it must be milk or nothing, until the dogs' health began to suffer and I had my way.

Nor had he time for raw meat or for biscuits; the dogs must be fed on cooked scrag of mutton. But one day I put out a large tray of biscuits and a bowl of water, and together we watched the dogs enjoy themselves.

Then came their training, and here my poaching stood me in good stead, for I wanted rabbits, and gun and snare brought me all I needed.

I would take the dogs and a dead rabbit into a quiet field, tie a forty-yard string to the rabbit, walk away with it, and send it jerking about on the end of its line, and call on the dogs. Before long I knew just which dogs were keen enough to hunt for a kill; dogs good enough to hunt the rabbit on a course, for there was no electric hare in those early days but a stuffed rabbit, fastened to the centre of a sheet of galvanized iron. Many a laugh I have had at the shape of some of those rabbits.

The first course I attended was not circular as they are today, but straight. At one end stood the traps with a man waiting ready to lift the doors at a signal. At the far end was a shed, and inside the remains of an old car. Two men stood by it, to wind up the cable that drew the rabbit, on to the rear axle of the car, by turning the rear wheels. I have seen those men after three or four races, dead-beat; they earned the money they got the hard way. And though they worked for all

OF GREYHOUNDS AND TOYS

they were worth, many and many a dog had a ride home on the galvanised iron, busy with the 'rabbit' it had caught.

Later a circular course was constructed, with a double wire on pulleys to get the rabbit on to the run and back into the shed – and no sooner was it back than it had all to be pulled out again for the next race. The working was cumbersome and crude and so was the track itself, and more than one dog I have seen break a leg there, and more than one run the wrong way round to meet the rabbit coming in.

The best dogs on the course, we found, were those that had caught and killed a live rabbit; next time they went racing there was no holding them.

There were backward dogs who seemed at first to have no hunting instinct at all, though it was there all the time. When I met such a dog I would put him in a kennel away from the others, and starve him for twenty-four hours.

Then, having caught a fresh rabbit, I would take out the liver and smear the blood all over his chops till he looked most murderous; but by next morning he was sweet and clean. Now all he wanted was rabbit liver. I gave him pieces of rabbit meat, and then skin with meat attached – and the next creature that dog saw with fur, he was after it.

His training was not completed yet. I got another rabbit skin, made a disc of it with a hole in the centre, and baked it gently in the oven. Then round the edges I sewed in bits of lead, obtained free from the breaker's yard.

I took the dog out again to the field carrying my leaded skin. All that was needed was a piece of meat to go into it. I then threw it as hard as I could, and at a signal sent the dog after it. And how he enjoyed the chase, and the 'kill'. Anything wearing fur after that must look after itself, and very careful we had to be with the cats of the neighbourhood.

One day my employer, nicknamed 'Shallow', said he would come and see me catch the rabbits I supplied so freely. I told him there would be little sport watching, for I used no ferret. 'Borrow one!' he said, but in the end I had to buy one, and pay a good price for it, though today you could not buy the poorest specimen for several times that amount.

I put the ferret, together with a few purse nets, into the

Gladstone bag my employer used for carrying the takings on the racecourse.

Once arrived at Cuffley it didn't take me long to set up the nets. 'Now let's have the ferret,' I said. 'Shallow' passed over the bag, for he would never trust himself to handle so fearsome a creature. But when I opened it, there was the ferret, stiff and dead: 'Shallow' had sat back upon it during the ride, and the whole journey was wasted, for without the help of the ferret we could do nothing.

We bought another, and made a second visit: 'Shallow', his clerk, and four more of us.

This time I carried the ferret, and netted the holes hopefully.

I whispered to 'Shallow', whose bad feet hampered him, to stay at the top of the bank, while the rest of us stood round the bury. When I had located the bolt hole, such as every warren has, and where they so often are, in the thick of a bed of nettles, I signalled them all to stay quiet, and put the ferret in.

I glanced up. There was my employer, resting on a low bough, peering down into the nettles. Almost at once I heard the thumping of a rabbit, but none appeared; till suddenly out came one from a hole I had missed, right between the legs of the clerk. He let out a startled yell, 'Shallow' jumped, and next second down he came, headfirst into the nettles.

Now it was his turn to yell. His face was a sight to see. 'What have I done? What's happened to me?' he cried in the agony of it.

'Nothing! All you want is a dock leaf!' I said.

He turned to his clerk: 'Get me a dock leaf!' he roared.

The clerk stood there, nonplussed. Born and bred in city streets, he had never heard of one.

' "Shallow" will remember what they look like,' I thought as I hurried to pick some.

'I've got two rabbits alive,' I said to mollify him.

'They'll be enough. Come on, I want to get home. We'll course those two, let them go one at a time, and see what the dogs can do.'

A few days later, all was ready. Eleven dogs there were,

OF GREYHOUNDS AND TOYS

and the kennel-boys, all eager for the sport, waiting to slip the leashes.

I took one rabbit out a hundred yards into the field and set it down from the sack. And there it sat, dazed, lost and still.

'Let 'em go!'

Off streaked the dogs, off went the rabbit, straight for the hedge. But it did not reach it, for from the hedge a little terrier ran out and killed the rabbit with one shake – my little Brinnie: and the second rabbit he served the same way.

Up came my employer, picked up the two dead rabbits, and in disgust looked at his dogs. 'I don't want greyhounds,' he cried, 'I want Aberdeen terriers!' And until Brinnie died, he never failed to knock as he passed on a Sunday morning, and leave some titbit for him.

Later, I became friendly with a manager at the old Blackmore Course, and attending meetings there I came to see a little of what happened at such places.

'Bring the dogs over!' the manager would tell us cheerfully, and hopefully we went, only to find week after week that we were losing. It became obvious that we were racing against local champions.

The next time we were asked, I told the manager we didn't feel it was much good our coming over merely to lose.

'You've a good dog called Sadie, haven't you?' he asked.

We had, her training was not yet completed, but we knew she was fast.

'Bring her over,' he said, 'that dog will win!'

We decided to take her, and when I saw the competition she was up against, I could have laughed. I hurried over to 'Shallow'. 'We'll win this week,' I said gleefully, 'the rest look more like shorn retrievers than greyhounds.' He laughed now, knowing my fondness for exaggeration, but being a business man he was already counting the takings.

'Don't put any money on till I tell you – till I lay a bet!' he counselled.

Sadie went on to the board at Ten to One, an unknown dog.

Still 'Shallow' said, 'Wait a minute, don't put any money on till the dogs are in the boxes' – and when we looked round again it was too late – the boards were cleared. The racing manager had put ten pounds on Sadie, and stopped the betting: we had not a halfpenny on our own dog.

'Shallow' was bursting with rage. 'Quick, you,' he cried, 'and get Sadie!'

With a snatch I tore her from the walker's grasp, pounded for the enclosure railings, and over she went.

Then came confusion and bustle. 'Shallow' put Sadie into the car, bundled in himself with two others, and was off.

But I was the wrong side of the fence, with an ugly-looking crowd just behind. I didn't stop to argue, I went over the railings. Across the path that lay outside was the river: I took a header straight in, and swam across: 'And that,' I thought, 'is a lesson on dog-racing.'

I preferred training them.

Some while later my employer bought two small greyhounds from Ireland, for thirteen pounds apiece. He was disappointed with them, they were so very small, and full of nothing but play.

They would not look at a rabbit, and so he left them to neglect, which is always a bad master: and they went their own silly ways.

One evening I was there with them alone, except for 'Shallow', all the other dogs having gone out for their two-mile exercise.

'What shall I do about the end kennels?' I asked – that was where the Irish dogs were.

'Ah, leave them,' he said, 'they're not worth a candle.'

But when I had finished clearing up I thought I would give them a run after all, and went down to them.

'Shallow's' car stood in the yard, and as soon as the two dogs were free, they started to play, racing round the car. Their speed and beauty of action took my breath away. I gave them their walk, and put them back as if nothing had happened, but all the time I could see them in my head, going round that car in a flash. I had never seen a greyhound turn so fast in so small a space.

A day or two later I said to 'Shallow', 'Those Irish dogs, what are you going to do with them?'

OF GREYHOUNDS AND TOYS

'You can have them for a couple of pounds apiece,' he said, 'and their pedigrees with them.'

I told him to take the pounds out of my wages, and off I went to my cottage with the dogs, Black Wyandotte Farm and White Wyandotte Farm, and their ancestry.

I determined to do with them as I had with the other greyhounds. I put them into a shed and gave them nothing but water for a day, while I went out with the gun for rabbits.

Home once more, I gave their muzzles the liver treatment, and by morning found them clean once more, and only too glad to eat anything. I gave them the rest of the rabbit chopped up. Then I played with them with the rabbit skin, till they shook it and ran with it, and tried to snatch it one from the other.

Now they were ready for training with the weighted rabbit skin. Within days they went mad with delight and the joy of hunting as they saw me coming to fetch them. Within a week my daughter Alice was taking them out on a leash. Next I taught them to leave a box quickly when I lifted the shutter, with somebody shaking a rabbit skin in front.

They turned out to be two of the liveliest dogs I have known, and lovely it was to watch them in action. But I knew I could not afford to keep them. My family, already large, was soon to increase. Employment was hard to get even had I sought it. The fields and odd jobs just kept us going.

It was perhaps a month later that an old shooting acquaintance, a man with plenty of money, came to ask if I knew where he might buy a good greyhound.

'Yes,' I said, 'and a very good dog it is, but it'll cost you ten pounds in cash, and another five I want put on it at the unlicensed track in Edmonton.'

He pondered this, evidently decided that if I wished to back my own dog it must be good, and said he would buy it, and race it that week.

And so he did, and placed my bets with three different bookmakers. He might have taken almost any odds he liked, the greyhound looked so small.

Away from the trap went the little dog, led from the start, and was home an easy winner.

Seven races that dog won for its new owner, though never again at the same odds. A race-going gang would have bought him, but my friend refused to sell, feeling that the dog was too good for that sort of track.

There came the eighth race, and the little dog won that too, but having been brought home, collapsed and died. A vet was called and said the dog had been poisoned, but of course no one could say by whom.

The gang ferreted out what dog it was that had been winning with such ease, discovered that it had a brother, and came to my cottage to know what I had done with it, and whether I was willing to sell.

I told them I had it still, that it was keen to a rabbit and would come out of a trap. They wanted to know why I had kept so secret about the speed of the dogs.

I explained that I had taken them and trained them when nobody else would consider them because they were small.

In the end they bought the dog, at a good price, and then they begged the loan of a long net, to catch some rabbits in the country as they said.

I knew how much of countrymen they were, and guessed too that if once they laid hands on a net of mine, I should see it no more. I fished out an old net with no top or bottom line.

They took it readily and off they went, and Sally and I laughed as we thought of the fun they would have trying to put up a net that was useless.

Off the course there was trickery and deceit, and on the course too. I well remember a dog, Edmonton Schoolboy, a black greyhound, a pet of the house, that I was asked to take to a track in readiness for a race. With the dog I received a small bottle of whisky. 'Give him this,' I was told, 'he likes a drop and we often give it to him at home.'

Well, he had his nip, and off he went to the trap, and four others with him, for a hurdle race.

Edmonton Schoolboy could certainly run: he was off like a streak, and cleared the first hurdle like a swallow going over a hedge. His owner looked across at me and winked: 'Told you he could go,' he whispered, 'didn't I?'

OF GREYHOUNDS AND TOYS

But at the second hurdle the dog got two forepaws on the bar and was still there at the end of the race. I ran to lift him off; he was blind drunk. I was glad I hadn't given him all the whisky – I drank the rest myself.

Now, what with the river incident, the trickeries such as giving dogs a piece of meat before the race to spoil their wind, and the difficulty in those days of collecting the money if you did happen to win, I began to think more and more of quitting dog racing, and in the end I did.

Times were changing for me in other ways too. My rat-cottage had been condemned for years, though I had not been told of this when I came to live there.

One day a notice came from the Council, telling me to quit. I had nowhere to go, and off I went to make inquiries at the Town Hall. I wanted to know if they would lend me a tent. 'We've put your name on the housing list,' I was told.

I told them I was out of work, with no prospects of getting a job. Then, they said, I must go before the Committee. There I went, explained that I could not pay the rent for a Council house, and had my application put back three weeks, for the case to be investigated.

I was summoned again before the Committee, and asked how it was I found myself unable to pay a rent of fourteen shillings per week. I told them I was out of work and that to pay that sum would mean taking it from the children, and that I would not do.

Three times I was asked the same question first by one Committee member, then another, till a blind lady sitting there said, 'Why keep asking the gentleman the same thing? He's already told you he can't pay.'

I was told to wait outside, and being called in again learned that I was to have a house at five and ninepence a week, inclusive of electric light.

I accepted with alacrity, for this was cheaper even than my old condemned cottage, where I paid eight shillings a week.

Before we had time to move, we were paid a visit. The children had just arrived home from school a mile distant, when there came a knock at the door.

A gentleman said he had been sent to see my children. I

asked him in, and told the seven children to line up against the wall.

He looked them over with care. 'H'm,' he said, 'there doesn't seem much the matter with them.'

'No, sir, they're all in good health.'

Sally brought in the pot and placed it on the table.

'By the way, what's for dinner – the pot smells good.'

It was a stew of potatoes, onions and starlings, and the steam and fragrance filled the little room.

The gentleman bent over the pot. 'Yes,' he murmured, 'it does smell good. I could eat some myself.'

Sally put some on a plate, and showed him the small birdies.

'Starlings!' I said. 'I caught them on the dust-shoot here at Edmonton.'

He took his departure, saying only that we should be hearing further.

The new house was ready.

I moved everything myself, making four trips with a handbarrow to save the cost of a horse and cart.

Once inside, and the door shut on the world without, we felt we had walked into paradise. No draught from the shut door, no rats, no oil lamps, no gas, but electric light such as we had had only in our dreams.

I found the money for Monday morning's rent of five and nine. But with the next Monday came the news that our rent had been reduced by a shilling. For nearly six years we paid that sum, till my daughters began to grow up, and the eldest brought home her first wages. Then the rent was increased by a shilling.

The time came when I needed a bigger house. My family was now nine instead of seven. I had found employment. I could afford the rent for a four-bedroomed house, I took one, and live in it to this day. I knew that if times fell hard, as they may for any of us, I could always fill the larder from the good land about me.

As time passed, my mind and my hands turned again to the making of things: the making of toys for children, for to use my hands has always been a joy to me, and children I love.

I wanted wood. I knew I could never hope to pick up

OF GREYHOUNDS AND TOYS

enough waste for my needs. I looked round for a cheap market and found one on my very doorstep, in the Edmonton Council. The Second World War was over at last, and the Council had air-raid bunks for sale. I bought some. I stacked the back-garden with wooden bunks, till the garden was no more; and slowly they dwindled down, to reappear as sailing boats. I made other toys: Donald Ducks, Monkeys-up-a-stick, Acrobats. Nor did I forget my old friends the dust-shoot and the rag-yards, for often they yielded me materials I could not obtain elsewhere, and there was little I could not turn to account.

Then, one day among the rubbish on the dust-shoot I found a mould for making a lead soldier. I brought it home and turned out a soldier, and that small model fired my imagination.

Fortune favoured me.

I took a temporary job building a shed for a local man who had turned his business to the making of hair-nets.

There, in another shed, I came across hundreds of toy moulds. I knew that somehow I must have them. I asked if my employer would sell them, even if it meant pawning everything of value I had. No, he would not sell them, he said, but if I cared to complete the job and take the moulds as payment, he would be well pleased. So I built his shed for nothing. As soon as it was done, I hired a coster barrow for threepence an hour, and brought home the moulds. Some were made in France, moulds made in two halves; for solid toys, Red Indians, cowboys, zoo sets and farmyard sets. Then there were moulds for the making of hollow models, soldiers of yesterday and of today.

For these hollow ones I needed antimony for making the lead hard enough. I found it very difficult to buy antimony, yet worth all my efforts. Solid models used a great deal of lead. With lead difficult to get too, and costing me eighteen shillings a hundredweight, I preferred the hollow ones. With five per cent of antimony in the alloy I could make a pot of lead last for hours; the trickiest part was finding just the right heat over the gas ring on the stove; but I had found a great happiness again, for I was creating with my hands.

The soldiers were mounted, six on a card, and the card put

in a box, of which I bought a supply from a maker. Six soldiers and as many colours on each, and the whole sold for one and threepence.

Shortly before Christmas I paid a visit to Club Row, to see if I could obtain orders for lead soldiers, and secured them easily enough. 'We'll come down and buy the lot!' I was promised. Promises, some say, are made to be broken. Nearly Christmas Eve. A roomful of toys, nothing in my pockets, and no buyer. It brought to mind another Christmas when all the clocks and watches were ticking away, waiting for their owners to pay me for them. But now, I could expect no customer.

By two in the afternoon I was desperate. 'Sally,' I said, 'come on, we'll have to sell them ourselves.'

Sally had an old pram, one we had bought from a doctor, big enough to hold four babies. We loaded it with toys, and set out, not knowing where to begin, nor where we might end.

We started in Silver Street. Now I felt a sudden distaste for knocking at doors begging for custom, though I had done it often enough before on my own. 'You try first, Sally!' I begged. The next thing I knew, she was inside, and came out smiling. We sold out in that one street, for seeing how easily they went I joined in and did my share. It was still but five of the afternoon, so home I went and got the rest, and those we sold too. I counted the takings. By selling direct to the public we had made half as much again. We had money in hand, the trade looked a promising one; I decided to launch out in a bigger way.

There were still shop orders to complete; I found I was unable to cope with all the work ordered. I asked the children of the neighbourhood if they would like to come in after school and help me paint toys. They flocked in, and most willing helpers they were.

Luck still held, everyone seemed eager to help. One day when I was on the dust-shoot, a man asked if I would care to buy some tins of paint. I was always on the look-out for good cheap paint, quick-drying, and in the bright colours I used so much, yellow, and red, and pinks and green. 'They're all

OF GREYHOUNDS AND TOYS

here,' he said, 'a penny a tin.' Cellulose paint, at a penny a tin; it seemed little short of a miracle. I bought the lot.

I began to use it the very next evening. There were seven children that night, round the big kitchen table. Before them were the lead soldiers with their spray of khaki paint, all ready for the colours to go on. Pouch, eyes, belt, black for the gun, silver for the bayonet, every child had its own particular work to do, its own dab of colour to put on, so that by the time all had gone the round of the table, every soldier was finished, ready painted, shining and bright for the box.

After perhaps a quarter of an hour, I noticed a girl not painting. 'Don't you want to do it tonight?'

'I feel so sleepy.'

'All right,' I said, 'go home if you like.'

It wasn't long before all the children were looking sleepy: and then I realised what it was; the fumes from the paint in the hot room (for I have the countryman's love of a blazing hearth) had overcome them all.

Seeing the children so profitably employed, the mothers asked if they could join, but that was more than we could manage.

I paid the children every Friday, when they came with their cards to show how many hours they had put in. But little work could we get done on a Friday, for there also arrived a man with a barrow, with two tiers of sweets; and in the end Friday night was pay-night only.

The lead toys sold well, and still in my spare time I made wooden boats, fourteen from each wooden bunk. The sails came from the same source as my paint, for I bought the thrown-out stock of a factory, four tea-chests full of small paste bags, with one side plain, just right for making sails. Those bags lasted me for years, right on to the period when I had a pet shop, and sold gentles to help trade (for nobody can make profit from gentles). Those paste bags I gave away, for carrying home the gentles and for use as bait bags after.

You may feel distaste to think that so much came from a refuse dump, but truly one half of the world wastes what the other half needs, and had you seen the toys when they were finished you would never have guessed their origin. Waste lengths of cardboard, card boxes, odd pieces of wood, I used them all. I sanded over the wood, and made forts: I made them from card too, and they were manned with soldiers painted bright by the children; good strong forts, sold complete in the shops for eighteen and six.

Then I thought I would make a machine for cutting out my shapes for toys. Tools I had always loved, both to use and to make. I had been watchmaker, sewing-machine repairer; I had worked with tools in an aircraft factory; working with my hands came easy, from repairing a bird cage to making a snare or fashioning a hammer for a gun from the solid metal.

I bought the machine I saw could be made to do the job – an old Singer treadle sewing-machine, converted it, and used it for many months till I was able to buy a lathe.

As time passed I began to understand that there was only demand for my toys at the right seasons, that after the Christmas rush, for example, it was no good expecting to sell sailing boats however good they were; they must await their season.

One good friend I had, who helped me by buying whenever I asked. To him I sold the first toys I ever made of plastic. When first I heard of this new substance, I hurried off to the library, and borrowed a book to read it up. One plastic, I learned, might be made from rosin and plaster of Paris. I bought rosin, melted it down in an old saucepan, and added my plaster. While it was still warm I rolled it out, and from it made a farmyard set, and some soldiers. Glued over, and painted, they looked very well. I took them round to my friend to show him: he thought they were excellent and gave me a good order.

It took me a week to complete it. He decided he would send some off to his wife, still living in the country whither she had gone during the war, and where she had opened a little shop. She made a fine show of them in the window, with plastic soldiers grouped around one of my forts.

One sunny morning a little boy came in to buy a soldier. He was back within half an hour, a ball of plastic in his hand – all that was left of the soldier.

The woman hurried out to look at the window into which the sun had been shining; one glance was enough. Some of

OF GREYHOUNDS AND TOYS

the soldiers were lying down, some were on their knees, some slumped drunkenly over their guns, but not one was upright: they were becoming mounds of plastic again.

I was sent for, and hurried over thinking a new order was on the way, but I soon saw something was wrong. My friend shook his head, showed me some of my gay soldiers, and asked what we should do about it.

'I'll replace every one,' I said. 'I'll make them in lead as it comes in.' This I did, and strengthened the bond of friendship between us so that he would allow no hard time to touch me. I had found a friend who believes that one good turn always deserves another.

A Poacher Dreams

TOYS, fishing rods and fishing gadgets: I made them all and sold them all, and in the end I bought a little shop. But I am not at rest in a shop, so that when the fever of the rush-times is over, I hate the four walls and the hours that make me prisoner. My only joy is in the people I meet, and the problems they bring. A girl brings her pet to have its claws trimmed. An old age pensioner comes with the bird that has cheered her lonely hours – a budgerigar shapeless with a tumour. A young boy carries in his first tortoise, infested with ticks. Fishermen come, old hands with cunning talk, and young lads afire with enthusiasm. They talk, and they get me to talking, and I spin them tales of the deeds we have done, my brothers and I, and those before us; fishing tales, and true tales of shooting and of poaching nights when I have lain within kick of a Keeper's boot, unguessed; of lying on the freezing ground, the wind biting numb down one side of my body, and on the other when I awoke, a hole burnt through my overcoat by the little fire I had made to keep life in me.

People come, and they go, and I dream of the old times. I see the pushing crowds in Club Row eager to buy the little birds I sold, I feel the soft spread of wing over finger; and as I sell, down the Row sound clear the notes of the Whistling King, a man who could whistle every bird song we knew, and all its variations, a man who would have made his fortune on TV today. Some men might trick and win for a while, like the man who rubbed down soft red brick and sold the dust as

Bug Powder, but the Kings of the Row were Kings in their own right, known to all, and respected by all.

The fields come back to me, and the long hours alone when I was never lonely.

I sit in a hedge with my flue nets hidden away till nightfall, for I mean to come again and take blackbird and thrush. They are coming in to the hedge now as the sky is aglow with the dying sun: I hear their soft notes as they drop into shelter. Then down the field sounds another note, 'Chizzick! Chizzick!' it grates on the evening; and farther away another chizzick and another; partridges, calling one another in to roost.

I make myself comfortable, push the last of the sandwich into my pocket, and listen, for tonight I shall learn where the partridges sleep. The calls come nearer, they sound close at hand, a partridge appears outside the gap where I sit. I stay without a muscle's move as one must, and watch from the corner of my eye that no glance shall meet his. He draws nearer, nearer still, and hop – he is on my knee, and over into the next field: and one by one the covey follows, each up on to my knee; I lose count they seem so endless in my intensity of excitement.

They are gone, and I listen for their whereabouts in the growing dusk: I hear them in the next field, twenty yards away, talking together as they prepare for sleep. I creep away so as not to disturb them, and go home for Syd. We come back with a traddle net, five feet high, held low to the ground as we advance up the field. Blomp! goes the first bird into the net, the one sentinel awake: over goes the net, and we take the whole covey. Cruel? Are we then more cruel than the man who would have shot them for sport?

I fall to musing again, of a time that can still wake me from sleep with a wordless horror.

I knew of a disused and derelict factory where in the autumn I had seen ducks fly over, but always too high for a shot. So I waited for a windy night when ducks fly low, and took the gun with me. I would get on to the roof, I thought, and once there I should be some twenty-five feet nearer, and within gun-shot.

I waited and waited, and saw dusk grow into half-dark then

into darkness, and no ducks came. Only the wind whistled and roared about me unseen, and set my nerves on edge. I climbed down in the gloom, and pieces of loose debris such as roofs seem always to hold scuttered down the roof and fell below and made me jump in the certainty of someone waiting for me there.

In the alley-way it was pitch dark, and there, what with the wind and the night and the noises everywhere around me, I lost my nerve. This was not the woods where I knew every sound, this was new and full of foreboding. I crept along the dark passageway and turned a corner towards the fields at the end. There was a side passage I must pass. I paused at it, gun at the ready, fearing for someone to leap out at me. No one. I peered round the fence. At the end of the passage-way was a building, and in a window the pale shape of a face. Without thought I raised the gun and fired. You would not have done it? Nor would I, in your circumstances, but I had lived with a gun till it had become as familiar, as automatic, as my right hand. A moment's reflection and I should have known I was safe, but I had no power to think because of the night and the gale: I fired to scare.

Now I stared at the building. No face! In a blind terror I ran for the fields and all the way home. I pushed open the door. 'I've shot a man, I've shot a man!' was all I could gasp to Sally. Someone I had to tell, but not the police, not any-one in authority. There began the most hideous week of my life. I hid within doors, venturing only to the Labour Exchange to draw money for Sally, expecting all the time to hear something, the word that would tell me the body had been discovered, that the crime was known. I hurried home, to wait for the knock to come. The gun I could not bear to look upon.

Then, as the week went by another urge came upon me: I must go back; see for myself. I should be caught, for they would be waiting for me, but back I must go.

With the coming of Sunday I crossed the fields again and made for the alley, sick with apprehension. I peered into the side passage: there was the window, shattered. I made myself walk along towards it. I wondered how the body would be lying. I must see. I drew breath and looked in. There was no body. Only a big enamel jug lying on the floor. I climbed in, on limbs that trembled. I picked it up; my hands were shaking too. The jug I saw with indescribable relief, was spattered with shot marks: this, was the man I had shot.

In the flood of relief I believe I ran all the way home again, seeing nothing and nobody, and burst out the news to Sally: and was a new man from that day.

The killing of a rabbit or a pheasant, that was nothing to me, I had killed them by the hundred, but I had lived with the terrible thought that I had killed a man, and I could not live with that thought. I had learnt the truth of the saying that a man will always return to the scene of his crime, no matter at what cost. From that week I count the beginning of the grey hairs that soon were to cover my head.

You may think that I would give up poaching after this, but I could no more help taking my food from the fields, than can the wild birds and the creatures that live their life there.

Yet no man fishes in the same stream twice. Time brings its own inescapable end to every tale: dusk must fall on every day.

It is a Christmas morning once again. We stand around Father's bed, in a hospital, waiting for him to regain consciousness. Nurses are singing carols in the ward. Father stirs: 'Listen,' he whispers, 'isn't that lovely, they're singing Christmas hymns.'

He stirred once again. A bird was singing in a tree outside. He roused himself and murmured, 'There's a thrush, singing to the spring.'

And so he died. On his body still, clear for all to read who might understand, were the scars made by a deer he had shot in Epping Forest and left for dead, and that had leaped up as he approached, lunged, and pinned him against a tree.

He had been poacher to the end, like his forebears, yet fair in his own way always to the birds and the creatures that he shot. In his own way too, he loved all living things, and within him dwelt the true sportsman.

He died as he had lived, a man unafraid of death. He had taken so many lives, he saw and believed implicitly in, death's finality. That he inflicted it before Nature's time, he saw as nothing wrong. He lived in an age when men believed in the duty of man to produce large families and then to keep them to the best of his ability. That which a man performed for the sake of his own, was for him beyond taint of reproach. He brought us up to believe in family life. One of his last injunctions to us was that we should meet together when circumstances allowed, and frankly discuss affairs: and if any should be in need, then all should help; and we remember his words to this day.

So the gun was stood in the corner for the last time, the snare laid upon the shelf, the fish went safe in their waters.

He was laid away from his own. The great bells of Waltham that rang over our heads as children ring no more over him, but he is not alone. The green breath of grass blows over his grave, the voice of the river whispers through the earth where he is laid.

What if there rings prophetic note in his passing?

I read the years in the glass, and in my brothers' faces; we are growing old together: the hand that never failed will tremble at the last.

But my family are all alive and well, seven daughters and two sons, and twenty-one grandchildren.

So if down the years you chance to meet with a sportsman or a poacher and find his name is Curtis, as it well may be, meet him as brother, for brother you have been coming with me through this book, and he will be living much of the life you read of here. Times change and fashions, and laws: but know this at least, that what he does, his inner self compels him to. He stands there alone in wood or field, nets hidden in the hedge, gun under arm, because the blood that pulses back through generations, runs hot in his veins. He is not alone for all his solitariness: time immemorial stands with him there: others, invisible, are with him, companions from the past. The life was born in him; as the twig is bent so will it surely grow.

14

Odd Thoughts and Explanations

SO many thoughts come to me now when the book is done, that I have felt I should put some of them down – odd memories, and comments on things I have said in the book.

I have told how Brinnie and I caught moorhens with wings frozen to their sides. Moorhens are not plucked, for then there is left the fine black down that kept them warm; they must be skinned.

The bane of our lives when we were bird catching was the sparrow-hawk. One had only to slide down the side of the wood or swoop over a hedge, and all our trouble was in vain. I have known a sparrow-hawk take a trapping-cage that was lying beside me on the ground, and carry it a field's length away, only to find it could not rise with it, nor could it reach the callbird within that had first attracted its attention. I kept a sparrow-hawk as a pet, and fed it on live birds – seeing no more cruelty in that than in having to kill the birds myself.

I have told too how wild birds grew wilder after an escape from capture. Some birds were so untamable as to be not worth the taking. The 'henriff' was one, an old cock linnet, quite untamable.

When we were after thrushes at roost, and saw one standing on one leg, we always declared it a cock, a theory upheld by so great an authority as Dr. Ludwig Koch. Speaking of bullfinches, Dr. Koch had one that sang a part of the Marseillaise, and then there was Desmond Hawkins's 'anti-Nazi bullfinch' that had been taught to sing the Red Flag. Alas, Hitler came to power, the owner of the bullfinch was denounced, and in order to save himself had to destroy his bird.

I had a bullfinch hanging by me when I was sawing, an old cock, practically untamable.

When it started to sing, all it would do was, 'See-saw! See-saw!'

I gave it to an uncle, but he brought it back within the week. 'Here,' he said, 'take this bird back, it's sawn up all the wood in my yard, already.'

Snipe shooting is tricky work. The snipe rises in a letter Z, goes ten yards straight and zigzags again. But many a shot loses his bird by hanging on. Watch the bird coming in, wait without move, hanging on neither to bird nor gun, then, up! bang! and the bird is yours. When we were after snipe in the winter days, we would often see little Jenny Wren creeping in and out of the holes in the ice above the ditch, going down for food.

I knew a large poulterer's where I could always dispose of plucked starlings. They were beheaded and each bird fitted with a snipe's head, then draped upon a dish with the head hanging over, and many a starling was sold, with the head removed ready for the next deluded customer. You are surprised that people should be so easily duped? No simplicity surprises me. I once sold a common mole to a townsman as a 'little wild pig'. Two moles put facing each other on a table will fight to the death, and a tap on the nose will kill a mole instantly.

People afraid of ferrets are bitten. They put a hand out gingerly, then snatch it away, with the ferret hanging to it. Come without fear and take hold from the back. Keep two fingers between chin and front legs and you are safe. The more they are handled the tamer your ferrets will become. You cannot expect much friendship from an animal that is half-starved and looked at for only a minute or so a day. A tame ferret is as affectionate and playful as a kitten. They are thirsty creatures and in the woods and fields when there was no water we would give them spittle to drink from our hands, and they would lick it up greedily. A line on a ferret except in the open is worse than useless, for where there are bushes, the animal goes under and over the roots till hopelessly entangled. If a muzzle is used, often with a tiny bit, to stop the ferret killing and feeding upon its kill, it scratches and tears at the cornered bunny, so that when at last you get it out, its back is bare.

With two ferrets, one a jill and the other a hob, put the jill in first, and she not wanting the attentions of the hob, will see that he is kept on the move. Some say tie a loop of string to the ferret's tail and the annoyance of it will send him out. We used to dab the feet with cotton wool dipped in turps, and the irritation kept the ferret on the move. To make a ferret release its victim, squeeze one of its feet. Look down at one in a hole, and you will see its eyes, bright as lamps. Put one in at a badger hole, and it will bush its tail out and stand eager, but refuse to enter.

If a ferret has gone to earth in a rabbit bury, and there is no other within fifteen yards, then he is cornered in that earth, for the next bury has no connecting tunnel, though a rabbit may dash out from one and go in at the other.

Rabbit snares are sometimes set by people who do not know, at the mouths of holes or in a hedgerow. I set mine some twenty yards out in the middle of a jump, that is, half-way between the little depressions in the grass that show where bunny landed. The snare is set, hand height, fingers spread, in a run, for a rabbit feeding out in a field always returns in haste to the run it has trodden before, and which it knows well, and where it travels fast. If the night is windy, steady the loop of the snare with a stem of grass, which the rabbit will ignore.

The snare we used is now illegal. Properly used, it strangled quickly, but set by a bungler it caused long suffering. But I have picked up rabbits caught in today's humane snare, with head swollen huge with blood where the creature had jumped again and again. The real torture of a snare remains – the terror a wild animal knows at being captive. A wild creature will endure terrible pain, even self-mutilation, and live, but the horror of the trap never goes.

The gin-trap we seldom used for rabbits, having little belief in it or need of it. Only for the bright kingfisher we looked out for a perching post, and there placed a round-jawed gin-trap, a practice long illegal though still used by Keepers at times for birds of prey. To catch a bird alive, we designed the trap so that it would spring to, but not shut tight. So it was that we were able to catch birds to feed the owl at the pub.

We bred tame rabbits. We would gather stinging nettles for feeding to them in the winter. We stamped the nettles down in a barrel, and filled in the top with earth to weight them down, and in the winter those nettles would cut like silage, and a fine food they were for the rabbits. We believed in simple country things, like the eating of perch to cure stomach ulcers.

A word or two now on some of the apparatus spoken of in the book.

Wing-nets or Clap-nets. A pair of nets, ten to eighteen yards in length. Only a skilled man could throw a long net, especially in stubble or on plough.

Clap-nets are always set with the wind blowing down the nets, for if it lies across them, one net will fly over fast, while the other hangs in the air, and all the birds are lost.

Never set nets where birds are feeding, but say two hundred yards away in an open field. There you must put some of the food they were eating into the nets. Then the birds, coming over, lured to the nets by the call-birds, will see the new supply of food, and come down at once.

Sometimes I would catch goldfinches without a brace-bird. I would make a dummy from a dead goldfinch, set it on a swivel and fasten it to the top of an umbrella spoke, and slip it in the thistles, with a thin string to the spoke. When I saw a bird in the air near by, I would pull the string a little to make the bird shift on its swivel to show the yellow and black of its wings – what bird-catchers called, 'flashing the bird'.

A chaffinch would never sit on the flirt stick, but always on the string behind it. When the string was pulled, it fluttered, and so flashed its wings, and down the others came into the net. Instantly you pulled the nets, for if the birds caught sight of the string they were off at once.

Half-over net. Half a pair of wings, laid in a 'furrow' cut in the grass, with one edge of the net pegged down and the rest folded over on top, so that almost nothing showed but two posts lying on the ground. Very good for the taking of shy birds.

Flue-nets. One foot to eight feet square, used for gaps in a hedge. Where the last blackbird, song finished, dipped in for the night, he would find our net. Used too for hawfinches, linnets, bullfinches, or any bird that used a hedge.

The net itself was in three parts, a centre section of squares, and two loose outer hangs of mesh. The bird flies into the net, its impetus carries it through into one of the squares, and it falls enmeshed as into a pocket, unhurt.

Half-hoop net. Used for birds that settled on the ground, from chickens to larks.

Net-board trap, a half-spring net to swing over to catch.

Long net, for rabbits. Nets sixty yards in length or more, four feet high, and with two-and-a-half-inch mesh. Every ten yards, the net must be given two yards of 'kill', that is, of slack. Then as the rabbit comes, head into one mesh and feet into another, and struggles to free itself, the slack holds it fast.

Back-net. A net held on two poles at arms width, rubbed over the walls of a house, over the ivy, to make the birds fly out. Bang went the poles together, and the birds were trapped. Used also for taking birds from a hedge at night, with the aid of a lantern.

Trapping cage. A small cage with a trap. Single trapping cage with no bird at the bottom; double and treble trapping cages, with extra traps for capturing birds alive at the top, and a call-bird at the bottom of the cage. Still to be bought in Club Row, openly displayed, despite their being illegal.

Call-bird. Birds to sing and attract others to the lure. I would take as many as seventeen birds at a time with me, linnet, chaffinch, redpoll, siskin. (For siskins we sometimes used a fishing rod with a spot of bird lime on the tip, and as the birds hung upside down in the hobs, the birches, we would reach up and catch them.)

Store-cage. A box with a wire front, with three holes for a small cage, or a row of them for a large cage, with drinkers attached. The cage had no doors, only holes in the top with a woman's stocking tacked around each, and tied with a knot at the top to prevent the bird's escape. Into the store-cage went our captures, perhaps seven dozen in one cage.

Brace-bird. A bird wearing a light harness of chamois leather from a woman's glove, and fitting the bird like a pair of braces. The brace harness was fitted with a tiny swivel so that the bird could not tighten up the brace in moving.

Flirt stick. In the clap-nets we used dummies, that is, stuffed carcases or skins set up with twigs to look lifelike. Sometimes the top line of the net would kill birds as the net came over, and these birds we used as dummies.

They were placed around a living bird, the brace-bird. This bird sat upon a thin stick, often a twig with the buds removed. The tip of the twig was whipped with thread, to give a smooth perch, and with a loop left for fastening the brace to. The lower end was hinged into a slot in a wooden peg, so that the twig could swing up and down, with the peg driven into the ground. To enable the catcher to move it at will, a thin line was tied to the lower part of the twig, and ran back through a hole bored above the swivel-slot, and so right back to the bird-catcher. A slight pull or give on the line caused the flirt stick to move, the brace-bird fluttered its wings, and drew the attention of the wild birds, who then saw the dummies quietly 'feeding' around.

Limed stick. Whale bone, fibres from bast brooms, or a stem of grass, kept in a tube filled with bird lime. The sticks had pins at the top. As one was drawn out the lime was smoothed, then 'snapped off' with a quick movement, and the pin stuck in where required. Used to capture birds flying at a dummy.

Bird lime. Rosin and boiled linseed oil mixed. Still to be bought ready made.

A few words on fishing, culled from the experience of my family, all fishermen, and winners of many cups, including the Philip Geen Cup, countless medals and money prizes.

Ledgering. The finest method. Fix a pear-shaped weight at the end of your line. Six inches back from the lead weight, fix with a tiny swivel a nine-inch line with the baited hook at the end. When the fish strikes, it pulls direct on the line, without shifting the lead, and the float or the rod-tip shows it at once.

Roach, bream, tench; bottom fishing. The method my six brothers use. On the line, one inch from the tip of the hook (which may be from No. 10 to No. 6), fasten a BB shot, heavy enough to take the float under if the weight is not on the bottom.

Now raise the float till it is cocking on the surface: the shot is resting on the bottom. When a fish noses the bait, the shot will roll and the float will wobble. When the fish picks up the bait, the float will jump and lie flat on the water; the bait is in the fish's mouth – so strike.

Pike and perch fishing. When these two fish are feeding, they are voracious, so that they will take anything that moves and is bright. But I find that the best bait in reservoirs is the perch for a pike or a small perch for a perch. I have told how some like to have the dorsal fin cut off, but this is wrong.

I said they are greedy feeders. I have taken a seventeen and a half pound pike on a six-inch gudgeon, and when I got it home, I took a pound-and-a-half bream from its stomach, with the head end partly digested. Yet, gorged as it was with a big fish, the pike had still to take another fish, even though small. What a glutton!

When a pike has been struck, do your best to keep it on a tight line, not giving it any slack. If you do, it will run out at great speed, and the jerk at the end of the line will surely snap it. Hold the line tight, so that as it strives to go out it can only travel sideways with the pull of the line, and steadily wind in. After a few runs up and down, he comes, quite sociable.

We used coarse lines such as are seldom seen in use today, since nylons came in, but they held.

When you are ground baiting a swim, before going to fish it, get a lady's silk stocking (I've made one of my daughters walk home with one on and one off). Fill it up with ground bait. Tie a piece of string on it, and throw it out, stocking as well. When the fish come, they seem unable to leave it, but stay waiting hopefully around that stocking, with very little feeding to take away their appetite for what you are going to offer them.

A few words to end with, on guns. They are meant to kill. It is no good saying afterwards that you didn't know; if you are going to carry a gun, it is your business to know. Good shots carry their guns safely, always.

Carry your gun – if over the shoulder, triggers uppermost, barrels pointing up.

If the gun is under your arm, make certain the breech is open, then the cartridges are safe and can stay in.

If the gun is at safety at half-cock, then carry it that way. That is what the maker intended. It takes only a split second to prepare for a shot.

When going through a hedge, empty the gun, or keep the barrels at safety with the hammers lowered so that twigs will not fire it off, and then keep the barrels up. Remember that snow or mud in a barrel means a burst barrel.

When walking with a friend, see always that he is behind your line of fire.

A good English gun is the best in the world. Many a young lad in the old days would start with a cheap Belgian gun, and in a month it was nothing but a box of clappers; you could rattle it. I have handled some of the finest guns made, and a good gun is a treasure to be looked after with infinite care.

I have used most powders and most shot. The Black Powder seldom used today was good on a windy day, for then you could see what you had shot, on a still day it was hidden by smoke.

I have many times pushed a rag into the muzzle, fired into the air and used the rag as it fell ablaze, to light a cigarette.

Black Powder, we always said, is a good medicine for a dog's skin troubles.

Black Diamond Powder we always considered very sharp, and had an instantaneous effect.

When we used to reload our cartridge cases, we would gather them from a pigeon-shooting match, re-size them and make them as good as shop ones. The little brass anvils we always saved for future use. If there was no powder for the caps, then we would put in a red match head, used also for firing muzzle-loaders.

Ballistite. Silver flakes of powder, which must be exactly measured. I once took a chance with it, and ruined a ·410 gun, a single, such as I always carried pheasant poaching.

Cannonite. I once loaded up five cartridges with this. I shot at a thrush leaving a hedge. The gun nearly came out of my hand. I killed the bird, but heard no sound for days after. I went home and took sixty cartridges to pieces to find which had the Cannonite, for they were muddled. Then I found I had opened the gun an eighth of an inch. Father was furious with the man who had sold me the powder without a warning. He took the rest of it to some allotments, and fired it. It seemed to lift the ground, made a hollow where it had been, and made an apple tree near by lean over.

Have I already told how powdered glass mixed with the powder is a good silencer? Shot mixed with Russian tallow would always carry farther before opening out, and killed at greater range.

We had to know how to kill, for the next meal often depended on it. Where in the tussocks of grass we found little feathers from ducks, we knew they would come to clean themselves after feeding – and we were there. We had learnt the maxim, 'Never point the gun except where you mean to kill.' Many a tragedy would be averted if that were only carried out. . . .

Well, our days came and went. Dawn saw us in the fields or trudging home, and the poaching life and the country ways were to us the only life we wanted; but to some the long hours of loneliness were more than they could stand.

One early morning I was bird catching in some hollows near to Cuffley. A young man was ploughing a field out of sight, but his fresh voice came on the quiet of the morning air, mingled with the clank and music of iron, and the calls of 'Gee-up,' and 'Whoah,' to his horses, and over and again his song, 'In the gloaming, Oh, my darling . . .'

It filled me with such unhappiness, in the end I went over to him and asked why he kept on singing it, and he told me the story.

He had met and fallen in love with, and married, a London girl, a dancer, full of life and fond of life, but the gay life of town. He had wedded and brought her here to live with him in the heart of the country, but the peace of it had driven her almost out of her mind, and she had left him. He loved her still, but hopelessly, and the happiness had gone from the fields and left emptiness, and in the singing was his only consolation.

SOMEBODY'S MOTHER

This is the poem I learnt at my Mother's knee, and which won for me the prize that followed me to the truant school. I have always remembered its lesson, 'Ever act kindly', and wish more people did today.

A. T. C.

The woman was old and ragged and gray
And bent with the chill of a winter's day.
The streets were wet with a recent snow,
And the woman's feet were feeble and slow.
She stood at a crossing and waited long,
Alone, uncared for, amid the throng
Of human beings who poured her by
Nor heeded the glance of her anxious eye.
Down the street with laughter and shout,
Glad in the freedom of school let out,
Came boys and girls like a flock of sheep,
Hailing the snowdrifts white and deep.
Past the old woman so old and gray
Hasted the children on their way,
Nor offered a helping hand to her,
The timid old woman afraid to stir—
Afraid lest the wheels or the horses' feet
Should strike her down in the slippery street.
At last came one of the merriest troops,
The gayest lad of all the groups:
He paused beside her and whispered low,
'I'll help you across if you wish to go.'
Her aged hand on his strong young arm
She bent, and so without hurt or harm
He guided her trembling feet along,
Proud that his own were young and strong.
Then back again to his friends he went
His young heart happy and well content:
'She's somebody's Mother boys, you know,
Although she's aged and poor and slow:
And I hope that somebody will lend a hand
To help my Mother—you understand,
If ever she's poor and old and gray,
When her only boy is far away.'
Somebody's Mother bowed her head
In her home that night and the prayer she said
Was, 'God, be kind to that noble boy
Who is somebody's pride and hope and joy.'